D1571398

DISCARD

A Daring Life

A Daring Life

A Biography of Eudora Welty

Carolyn J. Brown

UNIVERSITY PRESS OF MISSISSIPPI   JACKSON

Selby & Richard McRae
F O U N D A T I O N

www.upress.state.ms.us

Publication is made possible in part by a grant
from the Selby and Richard McRae Foundation.

The University Press of Mississippi is a member
of the Association of American University Presses.

First printing 2012

∞

Library of Congress Cataloging-in-Publication Data

Brown, Carolyn J.
A daring life : a biography of Eudora Welty / Carolyn J. Brown.
p. cm.
Includes bibliographical references and index.
ISBN 978-1-61703-295-0 (hardback) — ISBN 978-1-61703-297-4 (ebook) 1. Welty, Eudora,
1909–2001. 2. Authors, American—20th century—Biography. I. Title.
PS3545.E6Z59 2012
813'.52—dc23
[B]   2011051676
British Library Cataloging-in-Publication Data available

To Mary Alice, Liz, Patti, Suzanne, and Karen—
and all others who keep Eudora's candle burning bright

As you have seen, I am a writer who came of a sheltered life. A sheltered life can be a daring life as well. For all serious daring starts from within.

—Eudora Welty, "Finding a Voice," *One Writer's Beginnings*

Contents

A Daring Life

Eudora with brothers Walter (middle) and Edward Welty, circa 1917.
In later years, Eudora remarked that it was "[t]he first snow that I can remember."

Life in Jackson:
Eudora's Early Years

Learning stamps you with its moments. Childhood's learning is made up of
moments. It isn't steady. It's a pulse.

—Eudora Welty, "Listening," One Writer's Beginnings

Seeing a snowflake for the first time is one of these moments. Eudora Welty recounts this experience she had as a six-year-old elementary student in music class. She was living in Mississippi, in the hot and humid South, where snow was seldom seen, and she remembers how her teacher stamped this moment in her memory:

> [Miss Johnson] was from the North, and she was the one who wanted us all to stop the Christmas carols and see snow. The snow falling that morning outside the window was the first most of us had ever seen, and Miss Johnson threw up the window and held out wide her own black cape and caught flakes on it and ran, as fast as she could go, up and down the aisles to show us the real thing before it melted.

In 1909, the year that author Eudora Welty was born, Jackson, Mississippi, was a much simpler place, where snow falling was an exciting event, children ran after lightning bugs, and mothers baked bread, churned butter, and called the butcher and asked him to send over the best cut of the day. During her ninety-two years in Jackson,

Chestina and baby Eudora, 1909.

Eudora's first home in Jackson, circa 1907.
She lived there from 1909 to 1925.

Eudora witnessed close to a century of change in her hometown and state, but the year she was born, her family lived only two blocks from the state capitol and kept a cow behind their house. There were no modern grocery stores, and each household, Eudora recalls, "provided (ours did) its own good butter (which implies a churn and, of course, a cow) and its own eggs, and most likely it grew its own tomatoes, beans, strawberries, even asparagus." She recalls her childhood home on Congress Street in her essay "The Little Store":

> Two blocks away from the Mississippi State Capitol, and on the same street with it, where our house was when I was a child growing up in Jackson, it was possible to have a little pasture behind your backyard where you could keep a Jersey cow, which we did. My mother herself milked her. A thrifty homemaker, wife, mother of three, she also did

all her own cooking. And as far as I can recall, she never set foot inside a grocery store. It wasn't necessary.

Downtown Jackson in 1909 had a small urban center, but as Eudora remembers, "it was still within very near reach of the open country." Farmers brought their wares to you, and Eudora described "the old familiars" many years later in an essay about her hometown:

Many Jackson familiars were seasonal; and they were punctual. The blackberry lady and the watermelon man, the scissors grinder, the monkey man whose organ you could hear coming from a block away, would all appear at their appointed time. The sassafras man at his appointed time (the first sign of spring) would take his place on the steps of the downtown Post Office, decorated like a general, belted and sashed and hung about with cartridges of orange sassafras root he'd cut in the woods and tied on. . . . And when winter blew in, the hot tamale man with his wheeled stand and its stove to keep his tamales steaming hot in their cornshucks while he did business at the intersection of Hamilton and North West.

However, if Mrs. Welty discovered she was missing something from the pantry that she needed right away, she sent Eudora out with the correct amount of change in hand to retrieve it at the "Little Store" down the street.

"I knew even the sidewalk to it as well as I knew my own skin." The path to the "Little Store," as it was dubbed by the Welty family, was a familiar journey for a nine-year-old girl. Eudora remembers these trips fondly, especially the knowledge that her mother typically gave her an extra nickel to buy a treat for herself. "I'd skipped my jumping-rope up and down it, hopped its length through mazes of hopscotch, played jacks in its islands of shade, serpentined along it on my Princess bicycle, skated it backward and forward."

When she reached the store itself, on a block with family dwellings, and purchased what her mother had requested—a lemon or a loaf of bread—Eudora describes what it was like to spend the leftover nickel in the "Little Store":

Life in Jackson: Eudora's Early Years

Chestina and Christian, courting, West Virginia, 1903.

Chestina Andrews (standing, center) with her mother, Eudora Carden Andrews (Eudora's namesake) and four of her brothers (left to right): John, Moses, Carl, and Edward Columbus (Bus). The fifth brother, William Augustus, took the photograph at their mountaintop home near Clay, West Virginia.

Down at a child's eye level, inside those glass jars with mouths in their sides through which the grocer could run his scoop or a child's hand might be invited to reach for a choice, were wineballs, all-day suckers, gumdrops, peppermints. Making a row under the glass of a counter were the Tootsie Rolls, Hershey Bars, Goo-Goo Clusters, Baby-Ruths. . . . [Or] I might get a cold drink. . . . Deep in ice water that looked black as ink, murky shapes that would come up as Coca-Colas, Orange Crushes, and various flavors of pop, were all swimming around together.

For Eudora, running an errand for her mother was hardly a chore; on the contrary, a trip to the "Little Store" was pure joy: "The happiness of errands was in part that of running for the moment away from home, a free spirit. I believed the Little Store to be a center of the outside world, and hence of happiness."

Eudora's parents were not originally from Mississippi. They moved south from the North: Christian Welty was born in Ohio, and Eudora's mother, Chestina, lived in West Virginia. They met one summer when Chestina was working as a schoolteacher and Christian had come from Ohio to work in the office of a lumber company located nearby. She married Christian in 1904 in the home in which she was born, and he took her to Jackson, Mississippi, where he would eventually go to work for the Lamar Life Insurance Company.

From her mother, Eudora would get her strength, independence, and love of the written word; from her father, her passion for photography and travel; and from both a sense of adventure. Chestina, commonly known as "Chessie," was the lone girl in a family of six siblings; her five brothers were known as "the boys" and Eudora remembers from summer trips back to West Virginia the boys' love of music, singing together without accompaniment and hanging "their long-necked banjos . . . on pegs along the wide hall, as casually as hats and coats." Chessie was extremely close to her mother, as Eudora was to her, and it is from her grandmother, her mother's mother, Eudora Carden Andrews, that Eudora got her name.

Chestina Andrews demonstrated her strength and independent

spirit at an early age. She loved to read and she cleverly bargained with her father to obtain a treasured set of the works of Charles Dickens:

> Why, Papa gave me that set of Dickens for agreeing to let them cut off my hair. . . . In those days, they thought very long thick hair like mine would sap a child's strength. I said No! I wanted my hair left the very way it was. They offered me gold earrings first—in those days little girls often developed a wish to have their ears pierced and fitted with little gold rings. I said No! I'd rather keep my hair. Then Papa said, "What about books? I'll have them send a whole set of Charles Dickens to you, right up the river from Baltimore, in a barrel." I agreed.

Chessie's love for this set of books is legendary; as a young bride she brought the books with her to Jackson, and while she and Christian were living in a rental house it caught on fire. Chessie ran back into the burning house to rescue the books, throwing them out the second-story window. The books, now housed at the Eudora Welty House, still have the soot and mud on them from the fire. Eudora understands the amazing lengths to which her mother would go for a book, and wonders whether her love for her favorite book as a child, *Our Wonder World*, was as deep as Chessie's was for her Dickens: "One measure of my love for *Our Wonder World* was that for a long time I wondered if I would go through fire and water for it as my mother had done for Charles Dickens, and the only comfort was to think I could ask my mother to do it for me."

Chessie's other incredible act of courage occurred when she was fifteen and her father was ill and had to go to the hospital. The Andrews family lived on the top of a mountain in West Virginia and the closest hospital was in Baltimore, Maryland. It was winter, and as Eudora recalls in her memoir *One Writer's Beginnings*, "the mountain roads were impassable" on this particular "frozen winter night." With five sons at home, Mrs. Andrews remained and it was left to Chessie to accompany her father by raft to the train station where she managed to get him to the hospital in Baltimore. Sadly, it was not in time, and he died on the operating table from an infected ruptured appendix. He was only thirty-seven years old. In Eudora's version of the story, she describes the surgeon's shock when he tells fifteen-year-old Chessie Andrews to contact someone in Baltimore to assist her: "Little girl," he'd said, "you'd better get in touch now with somebody in Baltimore." "Sir, I don't know anybody in Baltimore," she said, and what she never forgot was his astounded reply: "You don't know anybody in *Baltimore?*"

After the sudden death of her father, Chessie was forced to grow up very fast. She had to help provide for her family and became a schoolteacher in a one-room schoolhouse, with several students older than herself.

With the money she earned teaching school, Chessie was able to attend nearby Marshall College in the summers and graduate with a degree. She did not continue teaching school after she married and moved to Jackson, but she shared her passion for reading with her daughter. Eudora was the Weltys' eldest child, but not their first. Christian and Chessie's first child, a son, lay in the nearby cemetery, having died at the age of fifteen months in 1907. Eudora reveals her discovery of her brother's existence when she found a small white box in her mother's bottom bureau drawer as a young girl. Curious, she opened it and unlocked its treasure: two shiny silver nickels. In her excitement, she rushed to her mother to show her what she had found.

Eudora remembers her mother's passionate "No!" upon seeing those two nickels in her daughter's hands. It was the discovery of the two nickels that prompted Chessie to tell her daughter about the brother she never knew.

[She] drew me to her, and told me that I had had a little brother who had come before I did, and who had died as a baby before I was born. And these two nickels that I'd wanted to claim as my find were his. They had lain on his eyelids, for a purpose untold and unimaginable. "He was a fine little baby, my first baby, and he shouldn't have died. But he did. It was because your mother almost died at the same time," she told me. "In looking after me, they too nearly forgot about the little baby."

This story, only told this one time, was stored away like the nickels in the memory of the story writer to be.

Stories heard and stories read filled the mind of the future Pulitzer Prize winner as early as age two. Eudora remembers her parents' book-filled home and the knowledge that "any room in our house, at any time of day, was there to be read in, or to be read to." She fondly recalls the books which were given on birthdays and Christmas, especially the ten-volume set of *Our Wonder World* she received at age six or seven. Lying down in front of the dining room hearth with volume five, "Every Child's Story Book," she read beautifully illustrated fairy tales by French and English writers, the Grimm brothers, and Hans Christian Andersen; myths by Aesop; and the legends of Robin Hood and King Arthur. Before she could read independently, though, Eudora imagines "I must have given her no peace," demanding for her mother to read at all hours of the day, even in the kitchen while she was churning the butter.

Eudora's love for stories was not limited to her mother's reading to her or reading to herself. She listened for stories, and this listening to elders began right in her own home and neighborhood. At night in bed, Eudora could hear her parents across the hall talking or reading to each other. "I don't remember that any secrets were revealed to me,

Christmas morning, circa 1914.

Eudora, Edward, Chestina, and Walter, 1917.

nor do I remember any avid curiosity to learn something I wasn't supposed to—perhaps I was too young to know what to listen for. But I was present in the room with the chief secret there was—the two of them, father and mother, sitting there as one."

Eudora's listening skills developed and her domain widened to include neighbors and even the old sewing woman, Fannie, who, Eudora writes, "spent her life going from family to family in town and worked right in its bosom." During Eudora's childhood, adults and children did not go shopping at the local Jackson department store for their clothing; "this was a day when ladies' and children's clothes were very often made at home." Eudora describes the process in *One Writer's Beginnings*: "My mother cut out all the dresses and her little boys' rompers, and a sewing woman would come and spend the day upstairs in the sewing room fitting and stitching them all. This was Fannie." Fannie was a talker, and despite her mother's protests ("Fannie, I'd rather Eudora didn't hear that"), could not be stopped from sharing the latest news. Eudora remarks that Fannie "didn't bother about the ear she was telling it to; she just liked telling. She was like an author."

Christian Welty holding baby
Eudora, 1909.

Eudora's father with his folding Kodak.

Eudora and her brothers playing on a cannon at the national
military park, Vicksburg, Mississippi.

The Welty family crossing the river on their annual summer trip to visit family in Ohio and West Virginia, circa 1916–1918. Eudora said that "Edward and I always got out of the car on the ferries to let the water run over our toes."

In 1912 Eudora's brother Edward was born, and in 1915 the Welty family expanded to include the youngest child, Walter. The family was extremely close and enjoyed many activities together, especially those suggested by Eudora's father, whom Eudora describes as a thoroughly modern man, a lover of "all instruments that would instruct and fascinate." For instance, a telescope lay on the library table on top of the maps, and the Welty family would gather after supper in the front yard "to find the moon and the Big Dipper . . . and to keep appointments with eclipses." In 1910, Christian carried his infant daughter in his arms to the window so she, too, could witness the passing of Halley's comet, and it was at the dining room table that the Weltys discussed the solar system and how the earth travels around the sun. Christian loved puzzles of all shapes and sizes, as well as magnifying glasses, gyroscopes, and kaleidoscopes. And it was Christian who introduced Eudora to photography, with his "folding Kodak that was brought out for Christmas, birthdays, and trips," a childhood hobby that later provided Eudora with income during the Depression.

It was Christian, too, who provided his daughter with her first dictionary, a *Webster's Collegiate*, "inscribed on the flyleaf with [my] full name (he always included Alice, my middle name, after his mother) and the date, 1925," which Eudora kept and continued to use her entire life. He also gave the future writer her first typewriter, a "little red Royal Portable" which she took to college with her.

Christian took the family on many trips, whether it was a daytime excursion to the military park in Vicksburg or further away to Ohio and West Virginia to visit grandparents, uncles, and cousins. For his daughter, he provided the greatest opportunity of her childhood:

Eudora in front of the Sunset Limited, the train she rode during a trip out west with her father, 1924.

a cross-country trip by train. Having worked his way up the ladder at the Lamar Life Insurance Company, serving first as cashier, then as assistant secretary, and finally as vice president, he organized a trip for his Lamar Life Insurance agents and wives in two chartered Pullman cars to travel to California. The itinerary included stops in New Orleans; Juarez, Mexico; and the Grand Canyon, before arrival in Los Angeles. The return trip included stops in San Francisco, Reno, Salt Lake City, Colorado Springs, and Pike's Peak. It was the trip of a lifetime for a fifteen-year-old girl and the beginning of a love affair with traveling that took Eudora to destinations far from her hometown of Jackson.

2

Eudora's Education

The pleasures of reading itself—who doesn't remember?—were like those of a Christmas cake, a sweet devouring.

—Eudora Welty, "A Sweet Devouring," The Eye of the Story

Eudora credits her parents for what she calls her "knowledge of the word," meaning her reading and spelling skills, because they taught her the alphabet at an early age. In *One Writer's Beginnings*, she describes how essential she believes the alphabet is as the cornerstone of learning:

> They taught it to me at home in time for me to begin to read before starting to school. I believe the alphabet is no longer considered an essential piece of equipment for traveling through life. In my day it was the keystone to knowledge. You learned the alphabet as you learned to count to ten, as you learned "Now I lay me" and the Lord's Prayer and your father's and mother's name and address and telephone number, all in case you were lost.

Her love of the alphabet itself came from reciting it, she says, but also from simply admiring the letters on the written page before she could identify them as words: "I fell in love with various winding, enchanted-looking initials drawn by Walter Crane at the heads of fairy tales. In 'Once upon a time,' an 'O' had a rabbit running it as a treadmill, his feet upon the flowers."

From admiring illuminated letters came learning to read, and Eudora recognizes, as she looks back at her childhood, the sacrifices her parents made to provide her with enough books. "Indeed, my parents could not give me books enough. They must have sacrificed to give me on my sixth or seventh birthday—it was after I became a reader for myself—the ten-volume set of *Our Wonder World*." Like the "Little Store" that was a short walk or bike ride down the street, so was the library, and Eudora's mother quickly realized her nine-year-old daughter would need a library card. Chessie introduced Eudora to the wonders of the library, and it was on the shelves of the downtown Carnegie Library (today the main branch of the Jackson library is called the Eudora Welty Library) across the street from the capitol that Eudora discovered the "Series Books." Children today gobble up the seven volumes of Harry Potter or the hundreds of Nancy Drew; in the early decades of the 1900s children enjoyed series of books which included *The Wizard of Oz*, the *Five Little Peppers*, and the *Camp Fire Girls*. Her discovery of the "Series Books" at the Carnegie Library was a revelation for Eudora: "There were many of everything, generations of everybody, instead of one. I wasn't coming to the end of reading, after all—I was saved."

Eudora, in her petticoats, standing with her bike, 1920.

Summertime trips to the library were as exciting as trips to the "Little Store." Eudora describes how the librarian, Mrs. Calloway, wouldn't let a young girl past the front door without a second petticoat (young ladies had to be dressed appropriately), and "[s]he called me by my full name and said, '[Eudora Alice

Welty,] [d]oes your mother know where you are?'" Children were limited to two books only, and Eudora would put her selections in her bicycle basket and take a shortcut through the capitol lawn as she eagerly rode home. "I coasted the two new books home, jumped out of my petticoat, read (I suppose I ate and bathed and answered questions put to me), then in all hope put my petticoat back on and rode those two books back to the library to get my next two."

A former schoolteacher herself, Chessie recognized that Eudora had the necessary foundation for school. She knew the alphabet and loved to read. So, at the age of five, Eudora recalls, with the elementary school located directly across the street from the Weltys' house, "My mother walked across the street to Jefferson Davis Grammar School and

Eudora biking past Davis Elementary School.

asked the principal if she would allow me to enter the first grade after Christmas." And the principal, Miss Lorena Duling, replied, "Oh, all right. . . . Probably the best thing you could do with her."

Miss Duling ruled Davis School with an iron hand; according to Eudora, she was "a lifelong subscriber to perfection, . . . a figure of authority, the most whole-souled I have ever come to know." In *One Writer's Beginnings*, Eudora acknowledges the great number of schoolteacher characters in her fiction, and it was Miss Duling who stamped her mark on the writer's imagination first. Eudora describes how she managed the children at school:

Her standards were very high and of course inflexible, her author-ity was total; why *wouldn't* this carry with it a brass bell that could be heard ringing for a block in all directions? That bell belonged to the figure of Miss Duling as though it grew directly out of her right arm, as wings grew out of an angel or a tail out of the devil. When we entered, marching, into her school, by strictest teaching, surveillance, and order we learned grammar, arithmetic, spelling, reading, writing, and geography; and she, not the teachers, I believe, wrote out the examinations: need I tell you, they were "hard."

Despite Miss Duling's difficult exams, Eudora did very well in school. In Jackson it was common knowledge which children made honor roll and who didn't, as the daily newspaper saw fit to print the names and grade point averages of all students who earned that honor. In fact, city leaders gave free season tickets to summertime Jackson Senators baseball games to the children who made the honor roll. Eudora says, "I offered up my 100's in arithmetic and spelling, reading and writing, attendance and, yes, deportment—I must have been a prig!—to Red McDermott, the third baseman. And our happiness matched that of knowing Miss Duling was on her summer vacation, far, far away in Kentucky."

Success at school led to success outside of school. Ten-year-old Eudora submitted a pen-and-ink drawing entitled *A Heading for August* to the *St. Nicholas* magazine and won a silver badge, and at the age of twelve, she won the Jackie Mackie Jingles Contest and received twenty-five dollars along with recognition from the judges in the form of a statement of hope that she would "improve in poetry to such an extent as to win fame." This accomplishment was followed by the pub-

Eudora's pen-and-ink drawing *A Heading for August*, which appeared in *St. Nicholas* magazine and won a silver badge, 1920.

"A HEADING FOR AUGUST." BY EUDORA ALICE WELTY. AGE 10.
(SILVER BADGE)

lication of her first poem, "Once Upon a Time," at the age of fourteen in *St. Nicholas* magazine. *St. Nicholas* was a popular periodical for children that had published other well-known writers and poets in their youth, including Edna St. Vincent Millay, Rachel Carson, and Ring Lardner.

Once Upon a Time

"Once upon a time"—that sounds
A great long distance back from now,
But that is when our dear St. Nick
To our grandparents made its bow.

Oh, if those boys and girls of old
Could view this long, successful climb,
They'd wonder what St. Nick will be
When now is "once upon a time!"

Eudora published a second poem in *St. Nicholas* two years later entitled "In the Twilight" which won a Gold Badge, the highest honor awarded by the magazine.

In the Twilight

The daylight in glory is dying away;
The last faded colors are fast growing gray;
The sun nears the beckoning portals of night,
And leaves to the skies his long, ling'ring light.

The sunbeams have hid 'neath a sad, misty veil,
And softened to shadows—dim, silvery, pale.
The Queen of the Night shyly peeps o'er the hill,
And reigns in her radiance—soft, cold and still.

A lone cyprus-tree, with its feathery grace,
Casts delicate shadows, like old Spanish lace,

On the cool, trembling waters that meet the gray sky,
And the moon rules supreme in her palace on high.

What's remarkable about this early poem is Eudora's use of imagery: lovely similes and metaphors are employed to describe this twilight scene, writing devices that Eudora would put to brilliant use later in her fiction.

After sixth grade, Eudora left Miss Duling and Davis School to attend Jackson High School. Eudora, who was placed in the first grade at the age of five, graduated from Jackson High School at the early age of sixteen. According to lifelong friend and author Patti Carr Black, "It was Jackson High School that opened a new and broad avenue of publication for Eudora." During a compressed three years of high school, Eudora contributed several written pieces and "over twenty pen-and-ink drawings to *The Quadruplane* [the school's yearbook]." Eudora also submitted illustrations to the *Commercial Appeal* of Memphis and "at least five pen-and-ink sketches were published there from 1923 to 1925." In addition to her original artwork, she also was extremely clever, creating fictitious clubs and organizations. One was called the "Blinking Buzzards," and she sent out illustrated invitations requesting classmates to join:

> Dearest Mary Ellen,
>
> Fair one, prithee hark unto what I have to say unto thee. Upon this day there hath been organized a new club, "Blinking Buzzards," by appellation, and tis my plea that thee becometh a member. For thou hast a lean and hungry look, which be the motto of the club. Needless to say, I be the organizer. Prithee answer. Eudora, Chief Buzzard.

Thus, it is not surprising that she declared in a "What They Intend to Do" column for graduating seniors in the high school newspaper that her career goal was to be an "author."

The same year Eudora graduated from Jackson High School, the Weltys moved to a new house on Pinehurst Place, across the street from Belhaven College. This is the house Eudora would call home for the next seventy-five years. It was designed by the same Fort Worth

Eudora's earliest contribution to *The Quadruplane*, the Jackson High School yearbook, 1923.

One of Eudora's illustrations for the Jackson High School yearbook, *The Quadruplane*, 1925. This illustration served as a divider page for the sports section.

Eudora's illustrations for the children's page of the *Commercial Appeal*, Memphis, 1923–1925.

Eudora, age sixteen, posing in her cap and gown, celebrating her high school graduation.

1119 Pinehurst Place, circa 1925. This is the house Eudora would call home for the next seventy-five years.

Jackson's first skyscraper, the Lamar Life Insurance Building, circa 1925. This is where Eudora's father worked.

architects who built Jackson's first skyscraper, the Lamar Life Insurance Building. A Tudor revival, the house was modern for its time with its double-entry foyer, indoor plumbing, and bathrooms, both upstairs and down. Eudora said herself that she was given the best room in the house because she was the oldest child and the only girl. Christian and Chessie had hoped to give Eudora a baby sister, but sadly a stillborn daughter arrived prematurely the year before they moved and was quickly buried the next day. Just as they tried to keep the death of their firstborn son a secret, "Chessie and Chris never discussed this new loss with Eudora, Edward and Walter."

Eudora enjoyed her bedroom only briefly before leaving her new home and her hometown in order to go to college. College was the first step in her journey toward achieving her high school goal of becoming an author, and perhaps the first time Eudora asserted her independence. Her parents wanted her to stay close and attend Millsaps College in Jackson, but traveling with her family, especially in recent years with her father to New York, Chicago, and Los Angeles, instilled in her a desire to study further away. A compromise was reached and Eudora enrolled at MSCW, the Mississippi State College for Women, located in Columbus, Mississippi, approximately two hundred miles north of Jackson.

She spent two years at MSCW, continuing to write in all genres: poetry, plays, fiction, and journalism. According to Patti Carr Black, "Within five months of arriving on campus she became a member of *The Spectator* staff [college newspaper]." She also was elected the freshman staff representative for the MSCW annual, *Meh Lady*, submitting illustrations as well as taking photographs. These creative outlets were not enough, however. During Eudora's sophomore year, she started a humor magazine entitled *Oh, Lady!* with a group of classmates. The young women only published three issues, but Eudora contributed a comic poem as well as illustrations and cartoons. Many of Eudora's written pieces during her two years at MSCW were comic; she especially enjoyed writing parodies and spoofs. On one occasion, Eudora's sense of fun resulted in delicious results:

Eudora on the campus of the Mississippi State College for Women.

> Egged on by friends studying late, she explained to the [Hershey Candy Company] president that she and her classmates, in a poor college in Mississippi, were often hungry. Would the company consider their request for nourishment in the form of chocolates? In a few weeks, a large case of Hershey chocolate bars arrived. Although Eudora and her friends were triumphant and delighted, Eudora's mother was not amused on learning that Eudora had written to the chairman of the board of the Hershey corporation that she was hungry.

An illustration by Eudora for the masthead page of *Oh, Lady!*, a humor magazine founded in 1927 by Eudora and classmates at Mississippi State College for Women.

Despite the fun, after two years at MSCW the environment stifled and bored her. Marching drills, daily prayer meetings, and chaperoned excursions were a mainstay of everyday life, and Eudora had hoped for more. Eudora herself described life at MSCW as "life in a crowd":

> We'd fight to get our mail in the basement post office, on rainy mornings, surrounded by other girls doing the Three Graces, where the gym teacher would have had to bring her first-period class indoors to practice.... When we all had to crowd into compulsory chapel, one or two little frail undernourished students would faint sometimes—we had a fifteen-minute long Alma Mater to sing.

Freedom came in the form of a fire escape outside Old Main, the dormitory where Eudora lived, or occasional unchaperoned trips, despite the risk of dismissal, to such places in downtown Columbus as the

Gilmer Hotel dining room and the Princess Theatre, where she won a Charleston contest. She even walked fifteen miles to the vacant, abandoned antebellum mansion, Waverly, to picnic with friends. Two years in Columbus was sufficient for Eudora, and this time, with her parents' permission, she applied to two schools much further away: Randolph-Macon Woman's College in Lynchburg, Virginia, and the University of Wisconsin in Madison.

Eudora chose Randolph-Macon first, but upon arriving discovered that the school would not accept all her credits from MSCW. Her father suggested she take the train and travel directly to Madison to enroll there. She did, and finally entered an environment far different from anything she had known before. For instance, she compares the experience of taking art at MSCW and at the University of Wisconsin–Madison in *One Writer's Beginnings*: ". . . I walked into my art class and saw, in place of the bowl of fruit and the glass bottle and ginger jar of the still life I used to draw at MSCW, a live human being. As we sat at our easels, a model, a young woman, lightly dropped her robe and stood, before us and a little above us, holding herself perfectly contained, in her full self and naked."

Her professors were especially engaging, such as English professor Ricardo Quintana, who found Eudora's work "brilliant" and Eudora to be a student with "an unusually acute literary sense." From Quintana, Eudora reveals what she discovered within herself when reading certain poets. In the stacks of the library at the University of Wisconsin Eudora found a volume of poetry by the Irish poet William Butler Yeats, and she wrote about the experience in a fragment of a story included in her memoir:

"I read 'Sailing to Byzantium,' standing up in the stacks, read it by the light of the falling snow. It seemed to me that if I could stir, if I could move to take the next step, I could go out into the poem the way I could go out into that snow. That it would be falling on my shoulders. That it would pelt me on its way down—that I could move in it, live in it—that I could die in it, maybe. So after that I had to *learn* it . . . [a]nd I told myself that I would. That I accepted the invitation."

The experience I describe in the story had indeed been my own,

Incident

I found a 'bright and, curious key,
Made of twisted silver-
It hung on a nail in the highest tree
In the forest of dreams.

I took it down with eager hands---
Thought it beautiful;
Fairies twist the keys of silver
In the forest of dreams.

Through a night of stars did I try the key,
Tried it unceasingly,
But never a tree-door its magic unlocked
In the forest of dreams.

E. Welty

The Spectator, May 3, 1927

"Incident," a poem published in *The Spectator*, the newspaper of the Mississippi State College for Women, May 3, 1927.

A photo of Eudora from the Badger yearbook, the University of Wisconsin-Madison, 1928.

snow and all; the poem that smote me first was [Yeats's] "The Song of Wandering Aengus"; it was the poem that turned up, fifteen years or so later, in my stories of *The Golden Apples* and runs all through that book.

At length too, at Wisconsin, I learned the word for the nature of what I had come upon in reading Yeats. Mr. Ricardo Quintana lecturing to his class on Swift and Donne used it in its true meaning and import. The word is *passion*.

Eudora may have found passion and inspiring professors at Wisconsin, but she never felt quite at home there. In a 1941 letter to her literary agent Diarmuid Russell, she describes her years in Madison as a particularly difficult time in her life:

It was the first crisis of a certain kind in my life, and I was frightened—it was when I was sent to the Middle West to school. I was very timid and shy, younger than the rest and those people up there seemed to me like sticks of flint, that lived in the icy world. I am afraid of flintiness—I had to penetrate that, but not through *their* hearts. I used to be in a kind of wandering daze, I would wander down to Chicago and through the stores, I could feel such a heavy heart inside me. It was more than the pangs of growing up, much more, I knew it then, it was some kind of desire to be shown that the human spirit was not like that shivery winter in Wisconsin, that the opposite to all this existed in full.

She made friends, enjoyed her classes, and even published an eight-line poem, "Shadows," in the *Wisconsin Literary Magazine*, but biographer Suzanne Marrs writes, "Despite her classes, her writing, and her friends, Eudora never felt at ease in Madison." In 1929, after graduating with a B.A. in English, Eudora decided to return to Jackson and to the house on Pinehurst Place, uncertain of her plans and future.

3

The 1930s: Finding Her Eye and Her Voice

Writing "Death of a Traveling Salesman" opened my eyes. And I had received the shock of having touched, for the first time, on my real subject: human relationships. Daydreaming had started me on the way; but story writing, once I was truly in its grip, took me and shook me awake.

—Eudora Welty, "Finding a Voice," *One Writer's Beginnings*

Back home in Jackson, Eudora reunited with old friends and felt more at ease than she had in Madison. She found part-time work at the local newspaper, the *Jackson Daily News*, writing witty journalistic pieces. Several of her Jackson friends, however, had plans to enter graduate school at Columbia University in New York and encouraged Eudora to attend. She applied and was admitted in the fall of 1930 to Columbia Business School, the university's advertising and secretarial program, a practical course of study which assisted in gaining her father's approval of her move.

Eudora was quickly bored with the advertising/marketing curriculum, and engaged herself by auditing comparative literature courses, attending classes that her friends were taking, such as Abnormal Psychology, and enjoying all that New York City had to offer. Ranging from the Metropolitan Museum of Art to smaller galleries in Greenwich Village, from Broadway to Harlem, Eudora's education was broader than her course of study at Columbia. In her account of Eudora's youthful writings, *Early Escapades*, Patti Carr Black states

Eudora outside of Johnson Hall, Columbia, 1931.

Christian Welty, circa 1930.

that Eudora "was enchanted with vaudeville and went as often as possible to the famous Palace Theatre." According to Black, Eudora herself said, "I was the only college student who went to Broadway at ten o'clock on Saturday mornings and didn't emerge all day. I went every week, never missed a change of the bill." Friends originally from Jackson and even one of her closest from Madison, Felicia White, granddaughter of famed architect Stanford White, found permanent residences in the city, giving Eudora several "homes away from home." But the fun would come to an end. At the conclusion of the spring term in 1931, although she had hoped to find work in the city and continue her studies, she was called back to Jackson because her father, only fifty-two, was seriously ill with leukemia. He would not live through the autumn.

Chessie must have felt the same helplessness about Christian as she had when she was fifteen and her father had died in the Baltimore hospital on that cold winter night. On his final day of life, Christian was in the hospital and Chessie by his side; Eudora was the only child present to witness her father's last moments. It is a sadly beautiful and poignantly described scene in her memoir *One Writer's Beginnings*:

When my father was dying in the hospital, there was a desperate last decision to try a blood transfusion. How much was known about the compatibility of blood types then, or about the procedure itself, I'm unable to say. All I know is that there was no question in my mother's mind as to who the donor was to be.

I was present when it was done; my two brothers were in school. Both my parents were lying on cots, my father had been brought in on one and my mother lay on the other. Then a tube was simply run from her arm to his.

My father, I believe, was unconscious. My mother was looking at him. I could see her fervent face: there was no doubt as to what she was thinking. This time, *she* would save *his* life. . . .

All at once his face turned dusky red all over. The doctor made a disparaging sound with his lips, the kind a woman knitting makes when she drops a stitch. What the doctor meant by it was that my father had died.

My mother never recovered emotionally. Though she lived for over thirty years more, and suffered other bitter losses, she never stopped blaming herself. She saw this as her failure to save his life.

Eudora's father, Christian, shortly before his death.

Biographer Suzanne Marrs notes that "Eudora would be haunted by the loss of her dearly loved father and by the plight of her equally loved mother, who was racked with grief and guilt." She continued to work on her fiction during the remainder of 1931, but was unsuccessful in publishing any stories. She was offered a part-time job at WJDX, a radio station in Jackson founded by her father in 1929, and was asked to create a weekly newsletter, informing the community of the station's programs. According to Black, "She was the entire staff, compiling the schedule of the shows, writing feature articles and previews of shows, selecting interesting fillers, and penning her own column, 'The Editor's Mike.' The newsletter was a perfect forum for Eudora's word play, wit, wide-ranging interests, and satiric writing." For two years she remained in Jackson, working at WJDX, but, restless and unfulfilled, she returned to New York in 1933, comfortable with the knowledge that she could leave her mother, who was finally adequately coping with her grief.

The cultural offerings of New York City were just what Eudora needed after the last two difficult years at home. Despite being unable to find permanent work, she enjoyed concerts, plays, and art exhibitions. Eudora never lost hope during her search for a job in New York; her sense of humor is evident, expressing itself in job applications. For example, in a letter to the *New Yorker*, a magazine of which she was a fan and which would publish much of her fiction later, she wrote: "How I would like to work for you! A little paragraph each morning—a little paragraph each night." She applied to *National Geographic* as well, looking for secretarial work. But no jobs were to be had this time around in New York either, and she returned to Jackson in quest of employment.

In 1933 the Depression had taken hold, and times were tough not only in New York and Jackson, but throughout the country. Chessie had begun to take in boarders and give bridge lessons. Eudora supported herself and her family with a variety of part-time jobs: she wrote for the Memphis *Commercial Appeal*; she did some substitute teaching; and she took pictures for the Jackson Junior Auxiliary and a local dress shop.

Eudora on one of her many trips to New York City; this one was taken circa 1944.

Eudora holding a camera, 1940s.

Before Eudora found success as a writer, she considered a career as a photographer. What had first been just a lark, taking pictures of friends and often being the subject of their photographs, became a serious endeavor as she started to photograph the state of Mississippi and its citizens and develop her pictures in a home darkroom she set up in her kitchen:

> My brother Edward made me a contact exposure thing like a little box frame. Then I got an old castoff enlarger from the Mississippi Highway Department. I set up a darkroom in my kitchen at night with a red light to work by, and the enlarger clamped on the kitchen table. It had only one shutter opening—wide open—and the only way you could control or graduate the exposure was by timing it, which you could learn by doing.

In 1934, in a letter of application to Berenice Abbott, an instructor of a photography class at the New School for Social Research in New York, Eudora reveals that she has "photographed everything within reason or unreason around here." Although she was declined admittance to Ms. Abbott's class and she had no initial success in selling her early photos, she continued pursuing both her photography and writing.

The 1930s was the decade during which Eudora was finding her "eye" and her voice. Despite working several part-time jobs and living on a limited budget, she managed to carve out time to write and take pictures. In 1935, on another trip to New York to look for work, she brought her camera and shot photos of the city itself: unemployed workers, elevated trains, city streets, and protests. What Eudora saw during this trip to New York would later become the setting and subject of one of her early stories, "Flowers for Marjorie." Again, though, Eudora was forced to return to Jackson, unable to find permanent employment in the city.

The next year, 1936, proved to be a turning point in Eudora's career. Returning to New York during the first few months with new photos in tow, she stopped by the galleries of Lugene Opticians, Inc. Gallery manager Samuel Robbins, impressed with her photographs, offered her a solo exhibition. In March Eudora's success continued when two of her short stories were accepted for publication in *Manuscript* magazine. The editor, John Rood, responded enthusiastically to her submission of "Death of a Traveling Salesman" and "Magic": "Without any hesitation we can say that 'Death of a Traveling Salesman' is one of the best stories that has come to our attention—and one of the best stories we have ever read. It is superbly done. And 'Magic' is only slightly short of it in quality." Eudora's photography exhibition at the Lugene Galleries ran from March 31 to April 15 and was followed by publication of "Death of a Traveling Salesman" in the May issue of *Manuscript*. Eudora's joy over these two simultaneous successes is palpable, especially the publication of her first story:

That was a great day in my life because for the first time something was being looked at critically.

This was from afar, an objective point of view, and they liked it and were going to print it. I didn't care a hoot that they couldn't, they didn't pay me anything. If they had paid me a million dollars it wouldn't have made any difference.

I wanted acceptance and publication.

12

the last
in our series of "one-man"
exhibits is

●

eudora welty

●

march 31st - april 15th, 1936
photographic galleries
600 madison avenue
between 57th and 58th streets
new york city

The invitation to Eudora's first photography exhibition at Lugene Opticians, Inc., in 1936.

Eudora continued to pursue both writing and photography simultaneously. In June she published a story entitled "The Doll" in a college publication, *The Tanager*, and later in the year she heard from Samuel Robbins that his new business, The Camera House, would mount another exhibition of her photographs. Although her creative undertakings were finally being acknowledged, she was not reaping financial rewards from them and continued to look for work. Eudora would eventually be hired by the federal Works Progress Administration (WPA).

The WPA was created by President Franklin D. Roosevelt to generate jobs for people during the Great Depression. It offered opportunities to millions to carry out public works projects, including the construction of public buildings and roads, as well as arts, drama, media, and literacy projects. Eudora's first full-time job with the WPA was as a junior publicity agent. In a 1989 interview, Eudora explains that "junior publicity agent" referred to her gender and not her youth. She traveled with WPA senior publicity agent Louis Johnson and they went all over the state. She describes the experience in the introduction of her book of photos from this period, *One Time, One Place*:

Eudora as a WPA junior publicity agent. She is meeting a family from Rankin County, Mississippi.

I was sent about over the eighty-two counties of Mississippi, visiting the newly opened farm-to-market roads or the new airfields hacked out of old cow pastures, interviewing a judge in some new juvenile court, riding along on a Bookmobile route and distributing books into open hands like the treasures they were, helping to put up booths in county fairs, and at night, in some country-town hotel room under a loud electric fan, writing the Projects up for the county weeklies to print if they found the space. In no time, I was taking a camera with me.

Eudora described the job as tedious in a letter to her close childhood friend Frank Lyell, but years later, reflecting back, she recognized that the job allowed her to see her state in a new light:

I was so ignorant to begin with about my native state. I was in my early twenties. I had gone to MSCW [Mississippi State College for Women] for two years, and that should have taught me, because I met girls from all over the state.

But I didn't really get an idea of the diversity and all the different regions of the state, or of the great poverty of the state, until I traveled and until I had talked to people. I don't mean school-girls like myself that were at college with me, but *people*, you know, in the street.

And, in her free time, Eudora photographed these "*people . . . in the street,*" who graciously allowed her to take their pictures. The subtitle of *One Time, One Place* is *A Snapshot Album* because that is exactly what these photos are: unposed and real. Eudora describes her method: "I simply asked people if they would mind going on with what they were doing and letting me take a picture. I can't remember ever being met with a demurrer stronger than amusement." From a lovely lady simply looking at a dress in a store window to a carnival crew tak-

Window shopping, Grenada, Mississippi, 1930s.

ing a break from work to members of a Pageant of Birds at Farish Street Baptist Church, Eudora captured the lives and citizens of her home state with an original and sensitive perspective. In the same 1989

Pageant of Birds costumes, Farish Street Baptist Church, Jackson, 1930s.

interview, Eudora objects to the interviewer's question: "How did you entice [your subjects] to let you take their photographs?" She replies, "I didn't 'entice.' My pictures were made in sympathy, not exploitation. If I had felt that way, I would not have taken the pictures. . . . I have never heard from a hostile viewer, of either race, of North or South."

Eudora developed long-term relationships with a few of her subjects during her years of employment as a WPA photographer. One gentleman was referred to by his community as Mr. John Paul's Boy. He was a simple-minded fellow whom Eudora photographed in Rodney, Mississippi. Eudora recalls that "the whole of Rodney looked after

"Village Pet," Mr. John Paul's Boy, Rodney, Mississippi, 1930s.

him" and "he showed me the church, and where the post office was." He revealed to Eudora that he would go to the post office every day to see if he had a letter, but "he'd never got a letter in his life." After she left Rodney and for years afterward, Eudora would send him cards.

Her WPA job assignments provided not only photography opportunities but subjects and backdrops for short stories and essays as well. The hotel in the short story "The Hitch-Hikers," she reveals, is "a perfect portrait of some of the hotels I stayed in"—no telephones or air conditioners, for instance. "The good [hotels] had electric fans in the summer. That was the only way you could cool off, before air conditioning. [And] no telephone in the room. You had to go to a landing or downstairs to the desk." And the subject of Eudora's short story "Keela, the Outcast Indian Maiden," came from hearing during a WPA assignment "about a little Negro man in a carnival who was made to eat live chickens." Her employment with the WPA would be short-lived, however. Six months later Eudora received her termination letter when the national office closed its Mississippi branch. Nonetheless, the loss of her job with the WPA at the end of 1936 was perhaps fortuitous as it allowed Eudora to focus fully on her own creative ambitions.

4

Before the War: Friends, Fellowship, and Early Success

"I haven't a literary life at all," [Eudora] wrote once. . . . "But I do feel that the people and things I love are of a true and human world, and there is no clutter about them. . . . I would not understand a literary life."

—From Katherine Anne Porter's introduction to Selected Stories of Eudora Welty

The loss of her job as a junior publicity agent for the WPA turned out to be a boon as Eudora entered her most productive literary period ever, publishing ten stories between 1937 and 1939 and exhibiting photographs in a second show at Samuel Robbins's new gallery in New York. Pulitzer Prize–winning author Robert Penn Warren, who was editor of the *Southern Review* at this time, recognized Eudora's talent and published six of her stories. Initially he had rejected Eudora's story "Petrified Man," but wrote back a year later requesting that Eudora resubmit it. Eudora, however, frustrated after it had been rejected the first time and then rejected elsewhere (she tells Tom Royals and John Little in a 1978 interview that "I had sent it all over to every magazine in the U.S.A., I guess, and everybody had sent it back"), had burned her only copy in the kitchen wood-burning stove and had no other copies of it. She did not respond after Warren's first attempt asking her to resubmit a year later; it was not until six months after that, when he asked a second time, approximately eighteen months later, that she sat down and retyped the story entirely from memory. "Petrified Man," an account of the gossip that takes place in a small-town southern beauty shop, appeared in the spring 1939 *Southern Review*, became an O. Henry Award winner, and is one of Eudora's most anthologized stories. It is considered a comic masterpiece.

In addition to "Petrified Man," Eudora published several other stories in highly respected literary publications during this incredibly productive period at the end of the decade. The *Southern Review* also accepted "A Piece of News" (1937), "A Memory" (1937), "Old Mr. Grenada" (later retitled "Old Mr. Marblehall") (1938), "A Curtain of Green" (1938), and "The Hitch-Hikers" (1939); and *Prairie Schooner* accepted "Flowers for Marjorie" (1937), "Lily Daw and the Three Ladies" (1937), and "The Whistle" (1938). In all of these stories, which would eventually be collected and published together under the title *A Curtain of Green and Other Stories*, Eudora begins transferring life experiences into fiction. According to biographer Suzanne Marrs, "What Eudora the photographer recorded on film, Eudora the writer recorded in memory. She did not, as she later told interviewers, consult her photographs when writing, but the memories of those photographic occasions stood her in good stead and would frequently appear in her fiction."

For instance, "The Whistle," about a young couple's attempts to protect themselves and their crop from the cold, was inspired by an overnight trip Eudora took in the spring of 1938 to her friend Dorothy Simmons's home in Utica, Mississippi. During the night a loud whistle awakened the women and when Eudora inquired as to the noise, Dorothy explained that the whistle sounded through the town to alert farmers to cover their crops due to cold temperatures. "The next morning Eudora looked out over fields covered with sheets and quilts, with clothes and bedclothes." For Eudora, the result was a story and "a new insight into the meaning of poverty."

In her essay "Looking Back at the First Story," Eudora confesses that "'Death of a Traveling Salesman' belongs to the family of all my stories in that its origin, its generative force, comes out of real life." She explains how she got the idea for the story:

> A neighbor of ours in Jackson in the 1930s, Mr. Archie Johnson, traveled that state for the Highway Department, inspecting and buying

up land for the right of way, and when he came back to town on weekends he would have some tales to tell. Mississippi roads in those Depression days were not numerous and were poorly kept up, all but unmarked. In remoter parts, to reach a householder not easily accessible by car, he would have to get out and walk. There was a fair likelihood of a stranger's finding the gravel or dirt road he was trying to reach somewhere on had simply petered out. Getting lost would have been easy: probably Archie Johnson couldn't have got entirely lost, but my imaginary R. J. Bowman could; and besides, Bowman had had the flu to weaken him the further for his defeat.

Another example of how Eudora turns experience into fiction is revealed in "A Curtain of Green." The garden Eudora's mother created at the house on Pinehurst Place became a source of comfort and joy for Chestina after the death of Christian in 1931. Chessie kept detailed and meticulous diaries of her garden, and one observation she made expresses her love of gardening as her unique artistic endeavor:

> Creating a garden is much like painting a picture or writing a poem, and artists and poets often make lovely gardens. But sometimes we less articulate folks who can neither paint pictures nor write poems, yet feel the need of expressing ourselves, find a garden a very happy medium.

In Eudora's story "A Curtain of Green," the main character, Mrs. Larkin, turns to gardening as a refuge after she witnesses her husband's sudden death and realizes that her love is ineffectual in saving him. This story, an exploration of grief and love drawn from personal experience, was honored in *The Best American Short Stories 1939.*

Chestina Welty working in her garden.

Eudora followed publication of "A Curtain of Green" with "The Hitch-Hikers," and it, too, is drawn from life. The main character is another traveling salesman, but very different from Eudora's first salesman, R. J. Bowman from "Death of a Traveling Salesman." According to Marrs, Tom Harris, the main character of "The Hitch-Hikers," may be modeled after John Robinson, a friend of Eudora's and her

John Robinson, on left.

first love. Eudora had known John since their days at Jackson High; at age twenty-eight he was now living in New Orleans and working as an insurance adjustor. He often returned to Mississippi on business and to visit family, friends, and Eudora. Tom Harris is a handsome and intelligent salesman, much like John Robinson, and moves throughout the Mississippi Delta as Eudora did on trips with John. The story followed "A Curtain of Green" with inclusion in *The Best American Short Stories 1940*.

In addition to John Robinson, Eudora was part of an extremely close circle of friends who all attended Jackson High School together. Four young men were especially close to her and they often gathered at Eudora's house on Pinehurst Place during summer evenings when all had vacation time or returned home. Nash Burger was a teacher at Central High School in Jackson; Lehman Engel was studying at Juilliard in New York but returned home in the summers; Hubert Creekmore moved back to Jackson after attending the Yale School of Drama; and Frank Lyell spent his summer vacations from Princeton back in Jackson. This well-educated and interesting group got together for game playing, conversation, and listening to music, especially classical and jazz. They dubbed themselves the Night-Blooming Cereus Club, after ladies in Jackson advertised that their night-blooming cereuses, a member of the cactus family which blooms once a year around midnight, would be in flower one particularly hot summer

Eudora Welty, Hubert Creekmore (holding branch), Margaret Harmon, and Nash K. Burger, Brown's Wells, Mississippi, 1936.

night. The group of friends joined in the fun to witness the annual event and from then on the title stuck. They took as their motto a line from a Rudy Vallee song altered to fit their needs: "Don't take it cereus [serious], Life's too mysterious." The club often met in a structure behind the main house that Eudora's brothers, Edward and Walter, built in the 1920s. There the friends gathered, playing games or taking humorous photographs of each other. Eudora describes the backyard clubhouse in a 1989 interview:

Eudora with Frank Lyell at Yaddo, an artists' colony in Saratoga Springs, New York, 1940.

In a little woods behind our back garden, my two younger brothers Edward and Walter put up what they called "the Hut"—scrap lumber, with hammer and saw. It was a little boys' neighborhood club, with passwords and all. I wasn't allowed in, but after they outgrew it, I turned it into what my friends and I called "the Pent-House." It was the Hut with its walls pasted over with photos out of *Vanity Fair*— our favorite performers in the New York theatre—Noel Coward, the

A night-blooming cereus
in bloom.

Eudora in the clubhouse,
1931.

Eudora posing in the clubhouse,
1930s.

Edward and Walter practicing their
building skills, 1922.

Lunts, the Astaires. We had our parties there. It was where I took photographs of my friends.

In this same interview, Eudora describes a typical party where she photographed her friends:

> Even when we had little dinner parties for each other with four or six people, we wore long dresses. And everybody came, you know, we came *as* somebody, like parties in *Vanity Fair*, people like Lady Abdy and the Lunts, all the people that Cecil Beaton photographed doing things at parties. We were doing our version of that. We didn't take ourselves seriously. We played charades, word games.

Eudora loved playing word games; according to Patti Carr Black, this group of literary, like-minded friends "played a variety of word games that they invented, including Who Were You With?, the Movie and Wine Test, Dullest Remarks, Cliches, and a favorite that Eudora invented, Old Magazines, in which they wrote dialogue balloons for photographs." This group also loved listening to George Burns and Gracie Allen on

Eudora playing at *Vanity Fair*.

the radio; going to movies to see the Marx brothers, Fred Astaire, and Katherine Hepburn; and attending concerts by black recording artists. According to Marrs, they were "the only white people present, [and] they sat in the balcony and relished the event." One of Eudora's most famous and narratively inventive stories, "Powerhouse," was based on a Fats Waller concert that she attended with girlfriend Seta Alexander in Jackson's city auditorium. Eudora, exhilarated from the performance, immediately went home and "transformed her impressions of Waller into fiction."

Eudora's friends were creatively minded as well, and together they inspired and entertained each other. One instance of this artistic fellowship was evident in an anthology of parodies compiled by Eudora, Frank Lyell, and Robert Daniel, a friend of Frank's from Sewanee. Daniel suggested the title, "Lilies That Fester," taken from Shakespeare's sonnet #94: "Lilies that fester smell far worse than weeds." This volume included parodies written by imaginary authors as well as phony biographies. Eudora recalled the "burlesque poetry anthology" in a tribute she wrote to Daniel in 1983:

> We did it entirely by mail; the edition consisted of one copy. Not long ago Robert ran across this, and when next we met he brought it out. We both still thought it was absolutely wonderful. The more so, maybe, when you see it now as the kind of pastime we all used to carry on, as a timeless *joie de vivre* that was a resource during the Depression.

Another important friendship that would last a lifetime was made during this period: in 1940 Eudora found her literary agent, Diarmuid Russell. Until this point in her career, she was sending stories out on her own, but publishing can be a tricky and complicated business, and Eudora was in desperate need of contacts. Not surprisingly, Eudora was quick to respond "Yes, Be my agent," when Russell contacted her on behalf of his new literary agency. Her quick reply seemed naive, and he cautioned her not to act too rashly: "Such promptness is not to be expected in this world. When one hangs out a shingle one has to sit down and wait—that is the tradition and business shouldn't come rushing to one. How do you know that we are honest or compe-

Diarmuid Russell, Eudora's literary agent (left) with agency partner, Henry Volkening, 1940s.

tent? We think we are but we never expected to be taken at our own word."

One reason for Eudora's quick response may have been that Russell stated in his letter that he was the son of the Irish mystic author, A. E. (George Russell), whom Eudora had discovered on her own in the library at the University of Wisconsin. In a letter to Russell in 1941, Eudora recalls discovering A. E. in the stacks of the library:

> It was just by chance, wandering in the stacks of the library, that I saw one of these books open on one of the little tables under a light. I can't tell you and it is not needed to, what it was like to me to read A. E. but it was a little like first waiting on a shore and then being enveloped in a sea, not being struck violently by a wave, never a shock—and it was the same every day, a tender and firm and passionate experience that I felt in all my ignorance but with a kind of understanding. I would read every afternoon, hurry to read, it was the thing the day led to, and at night what I had read would stay as my secret heart, for I did not let anybody there really know me. What you look for in the world is not simply for what you want to know, but for more than you want to know, and more than you can know, better than you had wished for, and sometimes something draws you to a discovery and there is no other happiness quite the same.

For Eudora, the contact must have seemed destined and right. Russell, of course, took the emerging writer on as a client and would serve as her agent until his death in 1973.

As Eudora's agent, Russell represented the author and looked to place her stories in literary and major national magazines, which he believed was critical to getting a publisher to accept a book of Eudora's stories. However, this was not his only role in her life: he became one of her closest friends and best first readers of her fiction. She let him know in a letter shortly after their agent-client relationship had been established: "If you keep telling me when what I write is clear and unobscured and when it is not, as it appears to you, then I will have something so new to me and of such value, a way to know a few bearings. Is this what was in our contract? I didn't understand it

Eudora was thirty-two when this photo for *A Curtain of Green and Other Stories* was published, 1941.

Katherine Anne Porter (left) with Eudora in 1940 at Yaddo.
Eudora recalled, "[T]hat summer I was reading the proofs of my first book and Katherine Anne Porter was writing the introduction, right across the hall from me."

would be so much." Russell was able to close out the decade of the 1930s with placement of two of Eudora's greatest stories in the *Atlantic Monthly*: "A Worn Path" and "Powerhouse." "A Worn Path" is the story of Phoenix Jackson, an old, courageous African American woman who journeys to obtain medicine for her grandson and braves all kinds of elements on her periodic trips to town. It earned an O. Henry Award and has become a standard and much-loved story for students and teachers of literature. Perhaps, more importantly, Russell was able to broker Eudora's first book deal: Doubleday agreed to publish a collection of her early stories, which would be entitled *A Curtain of Green* and include an introduction by fellow author and later close friend Katherine Anne Porter.

In addition to noted poet, novelist, and literary critic Robert Penn Warren, writer Katherine Anne Porter had noticed Eudora's stories much earlier. Two years before Diarmuid Russell contacted Eudora, Porter wrote a letter to Eudora stating she would gladly recommend the budding writer for a prestigious Guggenheim Fellowship because of her admiration for Eudora's "very fine work." In her introduction to *A Curtain of Green*, Porter continues her praise of Eudora's stories, commenting upon her natural talent and her skill in translating experience into fiction:

> She gets her right nourishment from the source natural to her—her experience so far has been quite enough for her and of precisely the right kind. She began writing spontaneously when she was a child, being a born writer; she continued without any plan for a profession, without any particular encouragement, and, as it proved, not needing any. . . . These stories offer an extraordinary range of mood, pace, tone, and variety of material. The scene is limited to a town the author knows well; the farthest reaches of that scene never go beyond the boundaries of her own state, and many of the characters are of the sort that caused a Bostonian to remark that he would not care to meet them socially.

Perhaps what is most remarkable, according to Porter, is just how "normal" Eudora's life is in Jackson, and the fact that she spends a great deal of time with her friends and yet is able to write as much as she does: "Normal social life in a medium-sized Southern town can become a pretty absorbing occupation, and the only comment her friends make when a new story appears is, 'Why, Eudora, when did you write that?' Not how, or even why, just when. They see her about so much, what time has she for writing? Yet she spends an immense amount of time at it."

However, the normalcy of her day-to-day life was to be severely tested in the decade to come: her brothers, Edward and Walter, her friends John, Hubert, and the rest went to war, and Eudora could no longer find the desire or time to write as she once did.

5
World War II: A Promising Career Interrupted

Do you think this at all—I am far from everything & mostly just think to myself—& I am no problem solver in my thoughts—instead I have mostly feelings & they are that the life, whatever it is for all of us, will in the end be the little, personal, everyday things—a personal matter, individual—I cherish that still & always—*Moments* will count, still, then—& be magical & colored, good & bad, as some little thing makes it—War & peace do not change that, do they?

—Eudora Welty, 1944 letter to John Robinson,
who was serving in Italy during WWII

Eudora had a large circle of friends, but her relationship with John Robinson seems to have become more intense during the years leading up to World War II. War was in the background of daily life now; Eudora writes to Diarmuid Russell that military maneuvers are becoming a distraction to writing:

Are big bombers flying all over New York and do they fly low, in under your desk? They do here, they fly under my bed at night, all those in the Louisiana maneuvers go over Jackson when they make a curve, and really one went under the Vicksburg bridge over the Mississippi River the other day, too lazy to clear it. I feel as if my bones are being ground to pieces but I suppose I will get used to it if I stay here for

Jackson is filled with air bases, air schools, air fields, and barracks and tents, a changed little place, loud and crazy.

Despite the noise, she managed to finish "The Wide Net," a story about a young married couple based on anecdotes John Robinson had shared with her. She even dedicated the story to him, "a mark, perhaps," according to Suzanne Marrs, "of their growing closer to commitment."

The attack on Pearl Harbor stopped, for a time, the success Eudora was having with her writing. Eudora was at the wedding of John Robinson's sister, Anna Belle, on December 7, and did not learn about Pearl Harbor until the festivities were over. Her life and writing were quickly disrupted as both her brothers and John enlisted following the attack. Worry about friends and loved ones consumed her, and writing fiction, says Marrs, "which had brought Eudora so much fulfillment, came to seem more and more apart from what mattered."

War disrupted Eudora's life in numerous ways. She was awarded a Guggenheim Fellowship in March 1942, but instead of being able to spend the year in Europe as many previous recipients had done and she had hoped to do when she had applied the year before, Eudora remained at home and wrote. She managed to write and publish "Livvie" in the *Atlantic Monthly* during this difficult year, earning another O. Henry Award for her effort. The war was a very real distraction to her writing, however, as John Robinson had joined the army air corps, Hubert Creekmore had been sent to Corpus Christi by the navy, and she was fearful and uncertain as to what the military might have in mind for her brothers. Between August 1942 and December 1944, Marrs states, "Eudora would write very little out of her experience. Worry, omnipresent worry, left her unable to write."

Edward left Jackson first, then Walter a month later, for military training. The house and neighborhood suddenly became very quiet, and Eudora sought to distract herself from worry and anxiety with travel, painting, and writing letters. She did not begin any new works of fiction, only saw previous labors realized or revised works for certain publication. She volunteered for the Red Cross, and even sought employment at the Office of War Information in Jackson, but no job was to be had. In addition to Edward, Walter, and John having enlist-

Edward in uniform.

Eudora and Walter.

ed, all members of the Night-Blooming Cereus Club were in service. Because her loved ones were serving in distant locations, she befriended soldiers stationed in the Jackson area, "treat[ing] these men as she hoped her friends, family, and the man she loved were being treated."

Until the conclusion of the war and the knowledge that John, her brothers Edward and Walter, and her Night-Blooming Cereus Club friends were safe and out of danger, Eudora would continue to have difficulty writing fiction. Two stories did, in fact, emerge from this period, "The Delta Cousins" and "A Little Triumph," both set in the Mississippi Delta, which led Eudora to the region in 1945 to do more research.

Eudora with Frank Lyell during the war, 1940s.

Robinson, still stationed in Italy, provided assistance and inspiration from afar as his Delta cousins hosted Eudora and shared the diaries of John's great-grandmother, Nancy McDougall Robinson, with her. These diaries were the link Eudora needed to connect the two individual stories and develop a novel. In *Delta Wedding*, the novel Eudora began in 1945 and published in 1946, Nancy McDougall Robinson's diaries of her life as a new wife in 1832 in the isolated wilderness of the Mississippi Delta provided Eudora with the background and history for the fictional Fairchild family. The novel, set in 1923, centers around the wedding of Troy and Dabney, but according to Marrs, Welty counted on her readers to recognize the "dramatic irony" of the work: "She and her readers knew that neither George nor Dabney, nor any of the Fairchilds would be able to remain in the relatively secure world of 1923. They would have to face severe economic depression and a world war. . . ."

Following the bombings of Hiroshima and Nagasaki, Eudora wrote to Russell that "I hope this ends before we have to do any more—before we drop another one. I am one of those that tremble about the universe—only you can't really tremble for a whole universe. In an H. G. Wells story, the scientists could have the bombs accidentally fall on their own heads and somebody would say, better that their secret died with them." And when it did finally end, Eudora rejoiced with other citizens of Jackson, taking to the streets and celebrating down-town, congregating on the grounds of the Governor's Mansion, St. Andrew's Episcopal Church, and in front of the capitol building. As soon as family and friends were home and safe, Eudora could return to her fiction.

With World War II over and her attention no longer focused on the global stage, Eudora closely inspected her own state and was not pleased with what she saw. In her opinion, Mississippi did not uphold the values for which the war was fought. She revealed her opinion in a letter to the editor of the Jackson *Clarion-Ledger* in December 1945: Eudora objected to the newspaper's lackadaisical coverage of Gerald L. K. Smith, a noted anti-Semite, who visited the state. She was ap-palled, and wrote the following letter to the paper:

Dear Sir:

Has any Mississippian bothered to inquire exactly what the fascis-tic Gerald L. K. Smith came to do in our state, and asked him to get out? Both Jackson papers today print unconcerned news accounts of this visit—a visit for which the word sinister could not be at all too strong—and let it go. No editorial comment, no questions asked in any quarter, it seems.

Nothing Gerald L. K. Smith could do is likely to be innocent, when he comes around poking his nose in, but this visit is not even pretending to be innocent. . . . Isn't there anybody ready with words for telling Smith that . . . we don't want him, won't let him try organizing any of his fascistic doings in our borders, and to get out and stay out of Mississippi? . . . [I]s there still nothing we can do to atone for our apathy and our blindness or closed minds by maintaining some kind of vigilance in keeping Gerald Smith away?

Angry and passionate, this letter in Eudora's hometown newspaper revealed a louder voice—one that would not sit back and tolerate the anti-Semitism, isolationism, and racism championed by legislators from her state. It was a very courageous position to take in 1945 in Mississippi, as the Ku Klux Klan was an extremely strong and real presence. Eudora told her agent, Diarmuid Russell, that in response to her letter she "got some phone calls of approval and 1 anonymous letter saying I was known as a dirty Communist and to keep my mouth shut," and Russell warned her to be careful because the Klan may be "out for your blood."

Eudora was not fearful as her attention quickly turned to John Robinson, home from war, and their relationship. A commitment did not appear to be forthcoming and he seemed depressed since his return. Thus, they parted for a while, although during this period she continued to write to John and even suggested joint projects on which the two of them could collaborate. However, any collaborative projects would have to be handled long distance: Eudora sailed for Europe in 1949 for a six-month tour of the continent.

Eudora's European tour took her to Italy, France, England, and Ireland. Traveling abroad she saw many friends and family, and eventually even Robinson, who had won a Fulbright scholarship and was studying Italian in Florence. In Paris, Eudora happened to hear a trio of American women sing, and met them following the show. Excited to meet a fellow southerner in a foreign city, the performers invited

Eudora sails for Europe on the *Italia*, 1949.

Eudora in Italy with William Jay Smith (front), Dolly Wells, and John Robinson (back), 1956.

Eudora and her friends to a Christmas party. Eudora gladly attended, but was keenly aware that attending a gathering given by African Americans was a faux pas of Mississippi social protocol, confessing as much to her Jackson friend Frank Lyell in a letter:

> After the Meudon party ... I dashed in on last train and went to party at the apt. of the Peters Sisters, colored singers with the A.B.O Music Hall. (This I didn't tell before, thinking wouldn't be so good for Jack-

son Xmas reports!—you would like this part though.) They are vast black ladies who do a wonderful show—there are 3 in the act, and 2 others and Mama, a California Unity Church member. She had made eggnog and potato salad and chicken salad—and they expected to throw a huge party, the tree all decorated, mistletoe hung, then had to go fill an engagement at a club at 2am, which is just when I arrived— and all put on baby blue velvet gowns and rushed out, I imagine the party began with most of the same guests when they returned at 6.

Eudora would violate Mississippi social protocol again by going out after the party with fellow writer Ira Morris to have a glass of champagne in a questionable establishment. Eudora did not care; all was fun!

When Eudora's European tour came to an end in June 1950, she found herself back in Jackson and living with her mother. At age forty-one, extremely independent and financially stable, Eudora sought to purchase her own house in which to live and write. However, again she met with societal obstacles, as the seller of the house she had hoped to buy refused to sell to an unmarried woman. Perhaps it was for the best, as Eudora set sail again for Europe for an extended time.

Eudora spent part of this European trip in Cork, Ireland, at the home of fellow writer Elizabeth Bowen. Bowen's home, a castle known as Bowen's Court, was more than just a place to stay; it was a way of life that suited Eudora: writing in the mornings; driving throughout the Irish countryside in the afternoons; dressing for formal dinners; and playing games and cards following the evening meal. But, even more importantly, Bowen herself represented an example of independence that Eudora admired; she shared a similar

Eudora, seated, on the grounds of Bowen's Court.

vision of the role of place in fiction and traveled between Europe and America freely and unencumbered. It was a wonderful friendship of similar types: both embraced "the writing life" and both, despite Eudora's recent discontent with Mississippi, felt rooted to their home place.

Following this tour of Europe, Eudora was settled back in Jackson now, happily content with her writing, traveling, and large circle of friends. Recognizing that after years of a roller coaster relationship with John Robinson a permanent commitment was not going to happen, she surrounded herself with friends and never looked back. As with the Night-Blooming Cereus Club of her youth, Eudora became ensconced in another tight group of friends: the Basic Eight. The core of this Jackson group was Charlotte Capers, assistant director of the Mississippi Department of Archives and History and later its head; Charlotte's assistant, Ann Morrison, and Ann's husband, Bill; and friends Jimmie Wooldridge and Major White. The seventh and eighth spots were most frequently filled by childhood friends and members of the original Night-Blooming Cereus Club, Frank Lyell and Hubert Creekmore, who returned to Jackson on a regular basis. The Basic Eight met every week, with a different member in charge of entertainment each time. Activities included continuing the tradition of the Night-Blooming Cereus Club by visiting Major White's home to watch the mysterious flower bloom; painting a mural in a stairway that led from the Morrisons' downstairs apartment to Charlotte Capers's house upstairs; traveling further afield, to Allison's Wells, an artists' colony twenty miles north of Jackson; or gathering for a picnic on the banks of the Mississippi River.

Elizabeth Bowen at work, 1950s.

With Diarmuid Russell at the helm and directing her career for ten years now, Eudora was extremely productive since she did not have

Eudora, along with (from left to right) Jimmie Wooldridge, Charlotte Capers, and Tom and
Seta Sancton, having a picnic on the banks of the Mississippi River, circa 1940s.

to worry about submitting her stories herself. She continued to ma-
nipulate the short story form, increasing a few of her stories to novella
length or writing interconnected short stories with shared places and
characters. It was clear that her talent for short story extended beyond
the typical boundaries. In 1949 Harcourt accepted *The Golden Apples*
for publication, a collection of seven connected stories set in fictional
Morgana, Mississippi; and, in 1953 she learned that Diarmuid Russell had not only signed a deal with Harcourt to publish her novella
The Ponder Heart, but that the *New Yorker*, a magazine in which she
had already published several short stories, had agreed to publish the
entire novella in a single issue. Eudora had only praise for Russell and
the feats he had achieved on her behalf: "It really is just marvelous
news and dazzles my head when I try to think about it till I'm not sure
I've taken it in. It was a feat you did—for sure—I'm more pleased
than anything that it worked out exactly as it came to you it might."

Life was rich and full for Eudora, and never boring. She continued to write and travel, spending extended periods in New York once
again. During 1951 her political voice reasserted itself when Adlai Stevenson ran for president. He was a candidate she was truly excited

about. She attended a rally and told her friend Frank Lyell, "All I can really think of today is election, and I feel if Stevenson is not elected we had all just better get out of the country. I feel so strongly moved by that man, think him so great. I've been mailing his speeches home, as of course none of them get printed down there." Stevenson, how-

The publicity photo taken for *The Golden Apples* by the publisher, 1949.

ever, did carry Mississippi, but lost the national election. Eudora, despondent, publicly expressed her sadness in a letter in the national publication the *New Republic*.

Eudora's career was in high gear in the mid-1950s: after publication of *The Ponder Heart*, a New York producer wanted to adapt the novella into a play, and it made its way to Broadway and great success two years later. Eudora even made a surprise appearance as a member of the jury in the third act during a matinee performance. She traveled to England to deliver three lectures at Cambridge University, including one that was especially popular with her audience and on a topic close to her heart: the importance of place in fiction. Upon her return, she traveled extensively in the States, visiting universities to read and meet with students. And in 1955 she received the William Dean Howells Medal for Fiction from the American Academy of Arts and Letters. Life was moving quickly, but home would soon call her back: the decade to come would see the deaths of all her remaining immediate family members.

The 1960s: Personal and Political Unrest

> What I do in writing of any character is to try to enter into the mind, heart, and skin of a human being who is not myself. Whether this happens to be a man or a woman, old or young, with skin black or white, the primary challenge lies in making the jump itself. It is the act of a writer's imagination that I set most high.
>
> —Eudora Welty, Preface to *The Collected Stories of Eudora Welty*

Concern over the health of loved ones became Eudora's focus after the travel, awards, and success that highlighted her life during the first half of the 1950s. Chestina Welty's eyes were deteriorating and she suffered from food allergies, and both of Eudora's brothers were afflicted with arthritis. The fall of 1956 would see all three Weltys hospitalized briefly, and foreshadow more serious health complications to come. Eudora needed all of her strength and was forced to put aside her writing intermittently as she assisted her brothers and mother.

A brief reprieve in 1957 that allowed for some writing was followed by the most demanding caregiving to date: both Walter and Chestina required Eudora's attention and aid. Walter was hospitalized again with problems associated with his arthritis, and frequently, while he and his wife, Mittie, consulted specialists regarding his condition, Eudora kept her nieces, Elizabeth and Mary Alice.

Following the Thanksgiving holiday in 1958, Walter went back into

The Welty family: Mittie, Mary Alice, Chestina, Eudora, and Elinor Welty (front); Walter, Edward, and Elizabeth Welty in back, 1956. Walter (top left) would die three years later.

Chestina Welty, 1950s.

Elizabeth (left) and Mary Alice in the garden, Easter, circa 1950–53.

Eudora with Elizabeth (left) and Mary Alice in New Orleans, 1950s.

the hospital and never recovered. Walter Welty died from complications of his arthritis in January 1959. He was only forty-three years old. Eudora wrote to her friend Frank Lyell after Walter's death:

> It's still incredible, all of it, & incredible that a disease like arthritis, that you hear of everywhere, that goes clear back to the Greeks, that so many people put up with in mild forms, could reach such devastating proportions, & in a young, healthy man—& could remain so mysterious—One of the research doctors said he hoped they'd learned something about it from this—which I guess is something.

Eudora with her mother.

Grief over her brother's untimely death was deep; even a visit from good friend and fellow writer Elizabeth Bowen, normally a source of great joy, failed to alleviate Eudora's pain. At the conclusion of her letter to Frank she remarks, "Heavens, Elizabeth Bowen passed through! Seemed so unreal I was about to forget to tell you."

Chestina's health deteriorated rapidly following Walter's death; she suffered a stroke, was now completely blind, and was understandably depressed over the death of her youngest child. For Eudora, putting her mother in a nursing home was simply not an option, however; Chestina loved her house and garden and there was simply too great a risk. According to Suzanne Marrs, "[D]angerously inadequate facilities and workers had frequently been reported by the national press. . . ." Eudora herself had described how wretched nursing homes could be in her 1941 story "A Visit of Charity." Eudora decided to keep her ailing mother at home and care for her herself, hiring additional caregivers to assist her.

That nursing her mother and her civil rights activism would become intertwined seems highly unlikely, but, in fact, that is exactly what happened during this same period that Eudora cared for her mother. Civil rights incidents were happening in Jackson and all over the South. For instance, Eudora was shocked by the presence of armed federal troops to enforce court-ordered integration of Little Rock High School, and expressed her dismay to Diarmuid Russell: "Such awful things happening, I feel like emigrating from the whole country. Bayonets!" She expressed her discontent quietly to her agent, but when the opportunity presented itself to demonstrate her political beliefs she acted without hesitation. When Eudora was invited to speak at Tougaloo College, an African American institution just north of Jackson, simply appearing on the podium was a courageous stance. It was very brave; by 1958 white visitors to Tougaloo had their visits monitored by the State Sovereignty Commission or its informants.

The unrest continued. In 1963 a professor and several African American students from Tougaloo College were asked to leave the nearby Millsaps College campus when they came to attend a play. Shortly after this incident, Eudora was invited by Millsaps to be the keynote speaker as part of the Southern Literary Festival and she requested that the college allow the lecture to be open to all (Eudora had friends at Tougaloo College that she knew would attend), and Millsaps agreed. Showing courage once again by reading to an integrated audience, Eudora concluded her lecture with her 1940 short story "Powerhouse," written years earlier after she had heard and was inspired by the music of Fats Waller. Reading this story to her interracial audience at Millsaps took great courage, as it illustrated, during this time of turbulence, how the power of music joins people together in a common experience and humanity.

Conditions on college campuses and around the country did not improve; on the contrary, violence became more extreme. In May 1963 a faculty member and a group of Tougaloo College students were beaten and one student arrested when they sat down at the lunch counter at Woolworth's in Jackson. And in June, Medgar Evers, secretary of the Mississippi NAACP, was assassinated in the front yard of his Jackson home. Shaken to the core by these tragic events, Eudora wrote her most political piece to date—"Where Is the Voice Coming From?"—the same night as the assassination of Evers. The story, written from the point of view of the white assassin, was accepted immediately by the *New Yorker* and elicited great praise from the editors, who recognized the enormous risk Eudora took in writing it. Eudora did, too, but as usual was not so much fearful for her own safety as for her mother's. Publishing a political story in a national publication like the *New Yorker* could certainly have a domino effect: publication leads to media attention, both local and national, which leads to reactions, both positive and negative. Eudora was extremely concerned about a hostile response to her story, as "such hostility would affect her ability to hire desperately needed caregivers for her mother."

Medgar Evers, secretary of the Mississippi NAACP. Eudora wrote "Where Is the Voice Coming From?" the same night as his assassination.

Fortunately, Eudora was able to continue finding satisfactory caregivers for her mother until Chestina's health problems became so severe that her physician required her to be placed in a convalescent home full-time in December 1963. The transfer of her mother to the Martha Coker Convalescent Home, located in Yazoo City, Mississippi, occurred immediately after the assassination of President Kennedy, a tragedy which shocked Eudora as it did the entire nation. As she had before, Eudora shared her most private thoughts and feelings about the assassination with close friend and confidante Frank Lyell: "I can't even start on the assassination—Like you I was glued to the TV—the whole weekend. Thought of you of course, in Austin where they were due just 3 hours from the time—Sickened and really awe-struck at what is now possible to happen."

Even though her mother was comfortable and well cared for at the center in Yazoo City, Eudora was still concerned over the civil unrest that plagued Mississippi and how it could affect her regularly traveling to visit her mother. She shared her worry and anxiety in a letter to her friend Mary Lou Aswell:

Mother is in Yazoo City, which is a little, rich Delta town with many more blacks than whites, and is reputed to be now the headquarters of the Ku Klux Klan. Our state is now authorized to get 200 more patrol cars on the roads and arm the highway patrol—just *one* thing. I hear that this summer all hell is going to break loose. Mother and I might even find ourselves separated—oh, it's frightening, I think, really. I want to get her away from Miss., but don't even know how to start, because first I have to find a place, find a way to transport her—with some nurse along, to travel—find a way to pay, find a new doctor— The poor, frail little thing, she begs me all the time to take her out of

"that hell-hole"—and it's the nicest place, newest, best equipped, best staffed of any in the Southeast, I believe—and anywhere she'd go it would be the same story.

Mary Lou suggested she bring her mother to Santa Fe, where she lived, but before Eudora could follow through on arrangements, Chestina had a setback and was not able to travel.

Eudora returned to writing on a fairly regular schedule once again, as well as visiting colleges as a guest speaker in order to help pay for her mother's care. She eventually took the only permanent teaching position of her career, at Millsaps College in Jackson, accepting employment as writer-in-residence. The job, arranged by close friend and chair of the English Department, George Boyd, made traveling less necessary and enabled Eudora to visit her mother as frequently as she liked. Students in Eudora's classes were carefully chosen, and she taught the class as a writing workshop. She described the class to her friend Bill Smith:

Eudora working with a student at Millsaps College in the 1960s.

My class at Millsaps college is with 18 young boys and girls, all bright and by no means all English majors—which I like—for instance, there are two French majors and both had been in Algeria, so when we came to Camus that was very informing for me too. I forgot to say that we have a book in the class and I chose Sean O'Faolain's paperback 'Short Stories' which is the greatest joy . . . The school is congenial—a number of the faculty are already friends of mine and among the liberals around.

As part of her teaching arrangement with Millsaps, Eudora took the stage again for another public lecture. Her presentation was similar to her first one: she was not afraid to speak her mind and read one of her pieces that clearly contained issues of race, making both a moral and political statement. Her title, "The Southern Writer Today: An Interior Affair," was a commentary on the purpose of fiction and later would be published under the title "Must the Novelist Crusade?" The answer is no, but the greatest fiction does not shirk its moral responsibility. According to Eudora, "What matters is that a writer is committed to his own moral principles. If he is, when we read him we cannot help but be aware of what these are. Certainly the characters

E. M. Forster, portrait by Dora Carrington.

of his novel and the plot they move in are their ultimate reflections. But these convictions are implicit; they are deep down; they are the rock on which the whole structure . . . rests." As an example, Eudora cited one of her favorite authors and novels, E. M. Forster's *A Passage to India*, praising it for the brilliant moral novel that it is: "It deals with race prejudice," Eudora says. "Mr. Forster, not by preaching at us, while being passionately concerned, makes us know his points unforgettably as often as we read it."

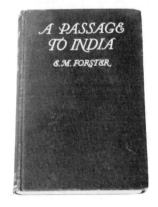

Eudora's copy of E. M. Forster's *A Passage to India*.

Eudora followed her lecture with a reading of her 1938 short story, "Keela, the Outcast Indian Maiden," about a clubfooted black man named Little Lee Roy who has been kidnapped and forced to perform as the title character. More importantly, the story addresses the guilt felt by Steve, the carnival barker, who takes responsibility for his role in this gross mistreatment of humanity. Marrs recognizes that by reading this story to her 1964 audience, "Eudora called attention to that guilt. She did not ask that her audience become political activists, but she did ask, implicitly, that they refuse to be part of racist activities, that they recognize the humanity and complexity of all individuals." And most significant of all would be the enormous step Millsaps College itself would take shortly after Eudora's lecture, three months later announcing that African American students were permitted to enroll. Five black students would be welcome on campus the following year.

Eudora was not done yet. She continued teaching at Millsaps throughout 1965, but, still frustrated by what she saw as a lack of any significant improvement in the civil rights arena in her state, she took to her pen again and wrote "The Demonstrators," sending it immediately to her agent and to *New Yorker* editor Bill Maxwell. Both Eudora's agent, Diarmuid Russell, and Maxwell loved it and couldn't wait to tell her so, but Eudora was unable to be reached. Two crises had occurred only a few weeks apart: Chestina Welty had a stroke and Edward Welty had broken his neck. Eudora tells Bill, "[T]hank you for liking the story, and for taking it. I am so glad. . . . Things are getting better but we've had a family crisis with two heads—my mother had a stroke and my brother, several weeks earlier, broke his neck and is in a hospital in Jackson—so they've been bad off fifty miles apart, and of course neither knowing about the other."

It appeared at one point during their convalescences that both Chestina and Edward would improve, but ultimately that would not be the case. Chestina died from complications of a stroke on January 20, 1966, followed four days later by Edward, who had developed a brain infection. Edward was only fifty-three. Eudora was now the only member of her immediate family remaining.

7

Grief and Recovery:
The Optimist's Daughter and *One Writer's Beginnings*

Of course the greatest confluence of all is that which makes up the human memory—the individual human memory. My own is the treasure most dearly regarded by me, in my life and in my work as a writer. . . . The memory is a living thing—it too is in transit. But during its moment, all that is remembered joins, and lives—the old and the young, the past and the present, the living and the dead.

—Eudora Welty, "Finding a Voice," *One Writer's Beginnings*

The double loss Eudora experienced in January 1966—the deaths of both her mother and younger brother—were sorrows from which she struggled to heal. Writing and travel, as they had previously in her life, provided much needed distractions; Eudora had many friends on whom she could count to help her through this difficult time, and they did—she took to the road for several months, visiting college campuses and stopping to see friends such as Charles Shattuck, Diarmuid and Rose Russell, and fellow novelist Reynolds Price along the way. When at home, alone, she returned to writing, focusing on the novel *Losing Battles*, which had been interrupted so many times during the last few years while she was preoccupied with the health issues of her mother and brother Edward.

In addition to the novel, Eudora wrote a long story, which she told

Eudora with friend and fellow writer Charles Shattuck, 1979. He was a professor of English at the University of Illinois.

her friend Frank Lyell "may be grim but [I] can't help it." Originally entitled "Poor Eyes" but later changed to "The Optimist's Daughter," it is considered by many to be Welty's masterpiece. In this extremely autobiographical story, the protagonist, Laurel Hand, is a young woman who, like Eudora, finds herself the last living member of her family. She travels back to her hometown in Mississippi to be with her father in his final days. In the home of her birth, she is haunted by memories of her dead mother and husband as she buries her father, all the while having to deal with her father's completely self-absorbed and childish second wife, Fay, and her family.

"The Optimist's Daughter" also deals with civil rights issues, a theme still much on Eudora's mind. In the story, which later would be revised and published as a novella, Laurel's father, Judge Clint Mc-Kelva, is remembered by his friends as courageous for preventing the lynching of a black man by the Ku Klux Klan. Eudora complicates the story, however, by questioning the collective memory of her father's friends, who may be making their dead friend more heroic than he actually was in order to cope with their grief. Laurel does not think her father capable of such heroism, but Eudora's point is not who is right, Laurel or the community: it is an examination of loss and memory and whether, as Marrs points out, "such memories provided false comfort to a white public unwilling to confront its collective guilt." In addition, Eudora beautifully illustrates the idea of memory and its power over Laurel as she recalls the deaths of those closest to her: her father, mother, and husband.

"The Optimist's Daughter" was accepted by the *New Yorker* and published in its entirety in 1969. It was also at this time that Eudora finally completed her novel *Losing Battles*, which she had started in 1950. *Losing Battles*, too, is very autobiographical; dedicated to her brothers, it is full of family stories told to her by her mother which had been passed down from her grandparents and are included as part of the lives and history of the Beecham/Renfro clan. Eudora was concerned that the novel, set in 1930s Mississippi, would not be critically accepted during this turbulent political period. To her surprise, however, it was enthusiastically praised, lauded by reviewers for the *New York Times*, *Life*, and *Newsweek*. Bolstered by strong reviews, the novel sold well and made the *New York Times* best-seller list.

With the novel behind her, Eudora's two closest literary confidantes, her agent Diarmuid Russell and *New Yorker* editor Bill Maxwell, encouraged her to continue working on "The Optimist's Daughter" in order to publish it as a book. She did, expanding it into a novella and developing more fully the section on memory and confluence and the character of Laurel's deceased husband. After extensive revisions, the novella was completed and published in 1972. It proved to be Eudora's greatest triumph, winning the Pulitzer Prize for Literature in 1973. Mississippi would recognize its Pulitzer Prize–winning author by declaring May 2, 1973, as Eudora Welty Day. Many of Eudora's friends as well as fellow writers would join her on this occasion, including Reynolds Price, Katherine Anne Porter, Ken Millar, and Diarmuid and Rose Russell. Eudora was greatly moved by the fact that Diarmuid would be there, as he had been in ill health for some time. She wrote close friend Ken Millar about Diarmuid's upcoming visit to Jackson: "Such a wonderful thing also happened in that Diarmuid Russell, who is ailing and frail,

The city of Jackson celebrates Eudora Welty Day, May 2, 1973.

has decided *he* is going to come. He and his wife Rose, for all the times I've visited them, have never been here to see me. I'm terribly moved." It would also be Diarmuid Russell's last task as Eudora's agent/editor; he would die on December 16, 1973, leaving Eudora again feeling very alone.

She dealt with this loss as she had with the loss of her mother and brother seven years earlier: with travel and writing, but more travel this time around. She went to Santa Fe and shortly after to Europe. According to Marrs, her letters from 1974 to 1980 "repeatedly stress her desire to seize the day." The deaths of her mother and two brothers, her agent, Diarmuid Russell, and close friends Hubert Creekmore, Elizabeth Bowen, and Dolly Wells relegated writing to a secondary place in her life: "Writing was not now Eudora's number-one priority. Human contact was." One of the highlights during this period was a return to New

Eudora with Patti Carr Black on the way to Europe.

Eudora in Paris.

York to see her own *The Robber Bridegroom* on Broadway for a limited run, but for eight years Eudora would be unable to complete any work of fiction. However, she had not ceased to write entirely: autobiography became the genre of most interest to her, as Marrs explains: "A writer's autobiography is most likely to be written near the close of a career, when intimations of mortality prompt the revaluation of experience. Such was the case with Eudora; her desire to seize the day did not wane, but her attention upon the past grew, and her focus on writing was renewed."

Eudora and Jim Lehrer, host of the television newscast *PBS NewsHour.* It was one of Eudora's favorite programs.

She embraced the autobiographical genre as she had the short story. Eudora was invited to give three lectures at Harvard in 1983 as part of the inaugural William E. Massey Sr. Lectures in the History of American Civilization and all would be primarily autobiographical in nature. Since she had won the Pulitzer and received both the Presidential Medal of Freedom in 1980 and the National Medal of Literature in 1981, Eudora's lectures were standing room only on the Harvard campus. Her former editor at the *New Yorker* and dear friend Bill Maxwell described the scene: "The audience was, for the most part, Harvard and Radcliffe undergraduates, many more than the hall could accommodate, with the overflow in other rooms that were wired with speakers. After the last lecture, bringing flowers, they waited in long lines for the privilege of speaking to her. Not bunches of flowers. Just one flower."

In addition to the recent awards Eudora had received, Marrs attributes her popularity to a flurry of media appearances and articles that followed the publication of her *Collected Stories* in 1980. Eudora had most recently appeared on *Today, Sunday Morning* with Charles Kuralt, the *Dick Cavett Show,* and the *CBS Morning News* with Diane Sawyer. A film biography about her life had aired on PBS, and interviews had been published in the *New York Times Book Review* and the *Saturday Review*. Marrs also thinks it has to do with her winning personality:

> Eudora's wry wit, her engaging sense of humor, her deft use of language, her penetrating observations, her love of home and family, her sanity and stability, had won her "friends" as well as readers. The response at Harvard partook of passion for her work and for the lectures she read, but also for herself. At a time when French philosophers Jacques Derrida and Michel Foucault were generating wildly enthusiastic responses from college audiences interested in literary theory, Eudora represented the antithesis of theory. . . . In her unassuming way, Eudora was charismatic. She represented high literature but in a down-to-earth, unpretentious, real, nonacademic manner.

The culmination of Eudora's Harvard experience was Harvard's desire to publish her three lectures.

These three lectures, which Eudora revised following her appearance at the college, were collectively entitled *One Writer's Beginnings* but individually titled "Listening," "Learning to See," and "Finding a Voice" respectively. What is most remarkable about them and most endearing are the stories straight from Eudora's life, especially the stories about her parents, grandparents, and figures from her youth. For instance, when she writes in "Listening" about a neighbor who rode in the back of the Weltys' automobile with Eudora's mother, Eudora describes this woman's flair for the dramatic:

> There was dialogue throughout the lady's accounts to my mother. "I said" . . . "He said" . . . "And I'm told she very plainly said" . . . "It was midnight before they finally heard, and what do you think it *was?*"
>
> What I loved about her stories was that everything happened in *scenes*. I might not catch on to what the root of the trouble was in all that happened, but my ear told me it was dramatic. Often she said, "The crisis had come!"

From examples, stories, and recollections such as these, Eudora explains how she learned to *listen*: "Long before I wrote stories, I listened for stories. Listening *for* them is something more acute than listening *to* them. I suppose it's an early form of participation in what goes on. Listening children know stories are *there*. When their elders sit and begin, children are just waiting and hoping for one to come out, like a mouse from its hole."

After learning to listen, Eudora explains how she "learned to see," devoting the majority of this lecture to reminisces of her parents and grandparents, and summer trips she took as a child. These trips, she realizes, were "stories" themselves:

> The trips were wholes unto themselves. They were stories. Not only in form, but in their taking on direction, movement, development, change. They changed something in my life: each trip made its particular revelation, though I could not have found words for it. But with the passage of time, I could look back on them and see them bringing me news, discoveries, premonitions, promises—I still can; they still do.

And, after her discovery that she could see them in this way and shape them into a written story, Eudora made a fascinating observation regarding time, with which she closes out this section of "Learning to See":

> The events in our lives happen in a sequence in time, but in their significance to ourselves they find their own order, a timetable not necessarily—perhaps not possibly—chronological. The time as we know it subjectively is often the chronology that stories and novels follow: it is the continuous thread of revelation.

These revelations about life and about fiction came with experience and reflection. Eudora's writing life and physical life were slowing down, and the remarks contained within *One Writer's Beginnings* display a mind and a life that have come full circle, the wisdom that comes from age.

In February 1984 Harvard University Press published *One Writer's Beginnings* and the reviews were outstanding. Papers all across the country sang its praises, and it remained on the *New York Times* best-seller list for forty-six weeks. It was a wonderful way to start the seventy-fifth year of Eudora's life; the success of *One Writer's Beginnings* was followed by a literary conference and celebration in Jackson during Eudora's birthday to honor the capital city's most distinguished author. Marrs describes the scene:

> In the midst of the publication hoopla, from April 12 to 14, Jackson, Millsaps College, and the Southern Literary Festival celebrated Eudora's newest achievement with a literary conference—scholars from around the country and from England and from France were present to analyze Eudora's fiction. . . . On April 13 [Eudora's birthday] conference participants and Welty admirers gathered for an elegant buffet supper; a smaller and more informal party, complete with belly dancer, followed at a local Greek restaurant with the unlikely name of Bill's Burger House. It was a fine seventy-fifth birthday celebration.

Eudora honored her hometown in return by giving a public reading and making a gift to the Mississippi Department of Archives and History. She gave her autobiographical and never-published novella, *Courtney,* written during her teenage years; five hundred Welty family photographs; and the typescripts and revisions of her three Harvard lectures to be part of the Eudora Welty Collection. With the establishment of this invaluable archive, "[S]elf-portraits and portraits, fiction, autobiography, and photographs would now be available for students of her fiction."

Eudora's seventy-fifth birthday cake. The author was also celebrating the publication of her memoir *One Writer's Beginnings* by Harvard University Press, 1984.

8

The Importance of Friendship: Eudora's Final Days

Lately, in my old age, it has seemed to me, when friends meet to hold a public service to pay tribute to one of their number who has died, that without words to that effect ever being said, they are drawing a circle around that friend. Speaking in turn one after the other, joining themselves together anew, they keep what they know of him intact.

—Eudora Welty, Introduction, *The Norton Book of Friendship*

The success of *One Writer's Beginnings* was followed by a whirlwind of honors and accolades for Eudora, celebrating a lifetime of literary achievement. Between 1984 and 1998 she received no less than nine honorary degrees, from such varied and prestigious institutions as Wake Forest University, William and Mary, Princeton, the University of Burgundy in France, and Mississippi University for Women. During this period, Eudora also was awarded the National Medal of the Arts from President Reagan; the French Legion of Honor, in a ceremony held at the Old Capitol Museum in Jackson; and was named one of "Ten Great Faces" by *People* magazine. In 1986 she bequeathed her home and all her papers to the Mississippi Department of Archives and History. These diverse awards and gifts marked the culmination of a distinguished career and popular life, but Eudora was not done yet. It is true that she seems to have had difficulty returning to fiction since the deaths of so many friends

Eudora receives an honorary degree from Wake Forest University in 1984.

Eudora receives the French Legion of Honor in 1996. She is flanked by French representatives who came to Jackson to give her the prestigious award in person. The award was established by Napoleon Bonaparte in 1802, and is the highest decoration bestowed by the nation.

Eudora's eightieth birthday celebration, 1989. Author Reynolds Price is seated beside Eudora.

and family members, but she still had two projects yet to complete. Suzanne Marrs suggests a few possible reasons Eudora could not complete any more fiction: "Perhaps she lacked the drive she had possessed as a younger woman. Perhaps her writing powers had waned, even though her intellectual acumen remained sharp. Perhaps she felt that her new work did not meet the high standard she expected of herself. . . . Whatever the reasons, Eudora did not complete any stories to her satisfaction."

What she did choose to work on was a new anthology on the theme of friendship and a collection of her photographs. These subjects suited her well at the end of her life, especially the friendship anthology. Marrs explains why:

> [F]riendships were at the center of Eudora's life; she treasured her friends, was absolutely loyal to and supportive of them, and found her own life enriched by these relationships. A book on this topic sparked her interest, and she was eager to work with [Ronald] Sharp. Eudora had found a project into which she could channel her creative energies, but which would not entail the physical and emotional demands of fiction writing. In so doing, she may have begun to recognize that her own fictional canon was complete. The time for writing fiction, she told interviewer Dannye Romine Powell, "may be forever away."

It was friendships that were helping her continue to lead a joyful life and, in 1989, the year of her eightieth birthday, Eudora was surrounded by friends to help her celebrate the occasion. She also traveled to New York for another notable writer's birthday—William Shakespeare's—and on April 23, the birthday of the bard, Eudora, along with twenty-six other notable women (Carol Burnett, Helen Hayes, Mary Tyler Moore, Toni Morrison, Leontyne Price, and Liz Smith, to name just a few) became the first female members of the formerly all-male Players Club, a club originally founded one hundred years earlier by the great Shakespearean actor Edwin Booth and numbering nine hundred *male* members. In an interview with the *New York Times*, Eudora said, "I'm stage-struck," referring to her admittance into the exclusive club; "I'm absolutely thrilled to be in the Players."

The happiness of these years can be attributed to her friendships and these two book projects. Eudora granted University Press of Mississippi permission to put together a book of photographs that she had previously donated to the Mississippi Department of Archives and History. Eudora also had agreed to be interviewed by the book's editors, and the interview, along with a foreword by close friend and writer Reynolds Price, would serve as the introductory materials for the collection. This book and the introduction she was writing and selections she was making for the friend-

The city of Jackson honors Eudora in its annual St. Patrick's Day parade, 1990.

ship anthology were keeping her busy despite increasing physical ailments and a continually busy social calendar in Jackson and out of town.

Eudora Welty Photographs was published in 1989, followed by *The Norton Book of Friendship* in 1991, and it was 1991 when Eudora's own health took a turn for the worse. Debilitating pain in her back prevented her from even getting up from a chair, and her niece Elizabeth discovered her in this painful state. Eudora was taken by ambulance to the hospital, her first trip ever to the hospital for herself. She was diagnosed with compression fractures. The fiercely independent single woman would no longer be able to travel or live on her own as she once did: she would require daytime sitters because the risk of a fall was too great. Marrs describes the great physical changes in Eudora's condition:

> From five feet ten or so, she was no longer even five feet four. Her arthritis had also intensified, leaving her unable to type, able to write only in the most cramped longhand, and unwilling or unable to shift to dictation as a method of composition. The compression fractures,

which had sent her to the hospital, presented an even more difficult physical challenge. They would mend, but their effects would linger. Eudora would ever after be considerably slowed.... Travel, for so long a cherished activity, would never again be a prominent part of her life. Neither could she, who loved driving her four-on-the-floor Olds Cutlass, ever drive again.

Fortunately for Eudora, she had Eddie May Polk, her housekeeper since the 1950s, who cooked, cleaned, and made Eudora's dresses, as well as Daryl Howard, who assisted Eudora with daytime activities, such as bathing, dressing, and driving. Daryl Howard remained with Eudora for the next ten years.

Her physical ailments may have slowed her down quite a bit, but Eudora still traveled with companions when necessary; for instance, she traveled with Marrs to Washington, DC, to receive three noteworthy awards: the Charles Frankel Prize from the National Endowment for the Humanities, the Distinguished Alumni Award from the American

Eudora and her biographer, Suzanne Marrs, at Mississippi University for Women, Columbus, Mississippi, 1989.

Association of State Colleges and Universities, and the PEN/Malamud Award for the Short Story. She received the PEN/Malamud Award a week after the other two, and felt well enough to make two trips to Washington in the same month and read "The Wide Net" at the award presentation. According to Marrs, "The reading and award presentation were originally scheduled at the Folger Shakespeare Library's rather small theater, but the demand for tickets prompted a move to a nearby church, which would seat six hundred people. There Eudora read to a sold-out audience."

Eudora granted a number of interviews during this period, too.

One interviewer, journalist Joseph Dumas, got Eudora to open up about writing and getting older:

> I think what I miss when I am not working is that I haven't got this thing to grip me; this piece of work that I want to lose myself in. . . . I can barely remember what I had for dinner. . . . It's a strange feeling. It's something that old people like myself feel often because you think back to the days when your familiar friends were around you and with whom you could talk and whom you counted and could discuss the nature of things; then you realize it isn't anymore.

Another interview Eudora granted was to Beth Henley, a successful playwright and fellow Mississippi native. Henley questioned Eudora about her story "The Worn Path" as a companion piece to a film of the story being shot by Hollywood director Bruce Schwartz. The director "felt that a production of the oft-taught story would have great appeal in high schools, colleges, and universities, especially if it were paired with an interview in which Eudora discussed the story." The interview proved to be extremely illuminating, and Eudora answered the question frequently asked about the protagonist's grandson: "Is Phoenix Jackson's grandson really dead?" The answer: "No."

Friends and family continued to come to Jackson to visit her, and Eudora's eighty-fifth birthday was an especially joyful occasion. During the week of her birthday, Eudora was at Lemuria Book Store in Jackson to celebrate her birthday, her life, and the publication of *A Writer's Eye*, a collection of her book reviews. A large crowd of family and friends gathered at the store, and tributes were sent and read from President Bill Clinton, news analysts Jim Lehrer and Roger Mudd, and former *New Yorker* editor William Maxwell, to name just a few. Just a year later, though, around her eighty-sixth birthday, "Eudora was more dramatically showing the effects of old age."

The effects of old age revealed themselves in the agony of compression fractures once again, and for the second time in her life Eudora was hospitalized. She was allowed to return home, but doctors' orders required that a hospital bed be installed and around-the-clock care be arranged. Eudora went home, but "[she] now faced a season of decline."

The last five years of Eudora's life were primarily spent on the first floor of the house on Pinehurst Street. Moving downstairs from her large bedroom, which was also the room in which she wrote, while looking out the window onto the lovely campus of Belhaven College (now University), was not an easy decision and was tinged with regret. It was necessary, however, as mobility was difficult. Although she had lost the ease of movement, her mind remained sharp until the final three years of her life. Marrs, who visited her daily during this period, recounts Eudora's gradual loss of memory:

> During these last three years, memory problems also intensified. Some days she was sharp of mind, engaged by the world around her, initiating conversations. Other days she seemed distant, her memory hazy. A change of medication for a time alleviated this difficulty, but by January of 2001, the bad days tended to outnumber the good ones. The recognition that her memory, her "treasure most dearly regarded," was failing must have been far more devastating than her immobility.

Eudora working in her bedroom. This photograph was taken about a decade before she was forced to move downstairs due to health issues (1970s).

The highlight of this year, Eudora's eighty-ninth, was the publication of the two-volume Library of America collection of Eudora's work. The Library of America series was established in 1979 "for the pur-

One volume of the Library of America collection of Eudora's work.

pose of preserving the best of American literature, works which scholars and literary critics feel might become hard to find or go out of print." Eudora was the first living author to be published in this series, joining such luminaries as Mark Twain, Washington Irving, Herman Melville, and William Faulkner. The publication of this distinguished two-volume set was marked by a star-studded event in New York City entitled "A Tribute to Eudora Welty." Writers who spoke included Richard Ford, Ann Beattie, Randall Kenan, Joyce Carol Oates, and Elizabeth Spencer. Marrs accompanied Eudora to the event and remembers the excitement of the evening: "The speakers and readers had been outstanding, the overflow crowd had been entranced, and the variety and virtuosity of Eudora's work had been affirmed—both as part of America's literary canon and in the hearts and minds of working writers."

Following this momentous occasion, Eudora was back in Jackson leading a much quieter life, and her ninetieth birthday found her simply at home with her niece, Mary Alice, Suzanne, and close friends Ann and Charlotte Morrison and Patti Black. At this point, Eudora's days could be labeled as simply "good" or "bad," and on one particularly good day, she agreed to the publication of the final book of her distinguished career: another collection of her photographs. Eudora's photographs of Mississippi cemeteries was published in 2000 and was entitled *Country Churchyards*.

In her final year, though, her ninety-first, the "bad days" outnumbered the good. Her memory was increasingly failing, and according to Marrs, "she knew me, as she knew her family members and other Jackson friends, but some days she did not know that she was at

Eudora's body lay in state in the rotunda of the Old Capitol Museum in Jackson. Many admirers and friends paid their respects to her remaining family members.

home. The house she had inhabited for seventy-six years seemed unfamiliar to her." In July of 2001, Eudora's deteriorating physical and mental state was complicated by breathing issues, and she had to be hospitalized. She returned home one last time, but the breathing problems did not subside, and she had to return to the hospital. On July 23, 2001, Eudora died of cardiopulmonary failure, surrounded by her family.

Eudora Alice Welty was given the highest honor bestowed on a citizen of the state of Mississippi: her body lay in state in the rotunda of the Old Capitol Museum where her many friends and admirers could file past the casket which contained her body. As no member of her immediate family remained, respect was paid to the closest living family members: her nieces, Elizabeth and Mary Alice, and their

Eudora's gravestone is in Jackson's Greenwood Cemetery. She is buried beside the brother who died before she was born.

husbands; her sister-in-law, Mittie; and her great-nieces and -nephews. The following day over six hundred people attended her funeral, including the mayor of Jackson, Harvey Johnson; the governor of Mississippi, Ronnie Musgrove; and a number of noteworthy authors. After the funeral, Eudora was laid to rest, and Marrs describes the location: "Burial took place at Jackson's Greenwood Cemetery, beneath a beautiful magnolia tree, next to the brother who had died before Eudora's birth, and within sight of the house where she had been born."

Afterword
Eudora Welty's House

During her lifetime, Eudora Welty donated manuscripts, photographs, correspondence, published works, and secondary works about her fiction to the Mississippi Department of Archives and History. The culmination of this great generosity came in 1986 when she deeded her home to the state of Mississippi, subject to a life estate interest. According to the Eudora Welty Foundation website, "in giving it to the State of Mississippi, she emphasized that it was the house of her family, a family that honored books and reading. She did not want a 'house about her' but about literature and the arts in culture." Eudora's house is a place where writers can be inspired and where visitors can enjoy the gardens that both she and her mother, Chestina, nurtured with such great love and care.

In 1999 the Eudora Welty Foundation was established to assist the Mississippi Department of Archives and History "in preserving and maintaining the Welty home and gardens and the Department's collection of Welty's photographs and papers." After Eudora's death in 2001, the house at 1119 Pinehurst Street in Jackson, where she lived for more than seventy-five years and wrote her stories, novels, and essays, was meticulously restored and named a National Historic Landmark in 2004. The home was opened to the public for tours in 2006, and "it is one of the most intact literary houses in America in terms of its authenticity."

When visitors enter Eudora's house, they do not feel as if they have entered a museum; instead, they feel as if Eudora has just stepped out for a moment. The house has been left to look as it was when

Afterword: Eudora Welty's House

The Eudora Welty House.

A sofa in Eudora's living room. Visitors would find books everywhere!

Eudora's living room. Her favorite chair is the floral wingback.

she lived there in the mid-1980s. Books can be found everywhere: on bookshelves and tables, and even on sofas and chairs. At the time of her death there were over five thousand books in the house! Friends and family have remarked that "they would have to move books when they came to visit so they would have a place to sit down." Tour guides point out Eudora's favorite reading chair, the many paintings of family members or those painted by friends or well-known Mississippi artists, and the interesting items that Eudora brought back from her travels or that were given to her by fans and friends.

The tour allows visitors to see firsthand how Eudora worked: she wrote at a type-writer in her bedroom in front of a window that looks out on the campus of Belhaven University. She did not face the window, but liked to sit where she could see outside. Her first typewriter was a manual, but she was forced to switch to an electric because of her

Eudora editing her work. The original "cut and paste."

arthritis. "She did not like it, however, and said it made a sound like it was 'waiting on you to do something.' (She never used a computer.)" She did her editing on the dining room table in order to spread the pages out on the table. She liked to cut paragraphs and sentences apart, rearrange them, and then pin them back together. It was "the original cut and paste, before computers."

Eudora's parents under a trellis in the garden, 1927.

A highlight of a visit to the Welty House is the garden, which has been lovingly restored and maintained to look as it was during the years 1925–1945. This was the period when Eudora worked alongside her mother. Chestina's journals, full of detailed descriptions of the flowers and seeds she planted, weather conditions, and how the plants thrived, along with Eudora's photographs from this time, have enabled the primary restoration consultant, Susan Haltom, to accurately re-create the garden as it was then. It was very important to Eudora that the restoration not turn her mother's garden into a "show garden"; Eudora's mother had been a schoolteacher, and "she viewed the garden as a learning experience—a living picture, always changing. She planned for continuous bloom throughout the garden." Thus, whatever time of year one visits, something is in bloom, whether it is the camellias (Eudora's favorite), the roses (Chestina's favorite), or the daffodils, irises, narcissus, spider lilies, or zinnias. Many, many varieties of flowers can be found here.

Inside the Eudora Welty House Education and Visitors Center.

One of the display cases in the Eudora Welty House Education and Visitors Center.

Since the opening of the house to the public, an Education and Visitors Center has been opened next door, with changing exhibits and programs. A gift shop offers many of Eudora's books for sale as well as prints of some of her photographs. Tours begin in the Visitors Center with a wonderful video of Eudora's life and then proceed to the house and garden. What is very special about visiting the house is that many of the tour guides are Jackson natives and have personal stories that they share about "Miss Eudora." A visit to Eudora's house is truly a literary experience unlike any other and not to be missed.

Acknowledgments

I would like to thank the following individuals for permission to quote or use materials in their possession: Liz Thompson and Mary Alice Welty White, Eudora's nieces, who spent countless hours with me, sharing photographs, reading drafts, and answering questions; Dr. Suzanne Marrs, my mentor, friend, and author of the definitive biography of Eudora Welty, who also shared items from her private collection, tirelessly answered questions, and never minded the occasional drop-in at her house; Karen Redhead, director of the Eudora Welty House, who also shared photographs, answered questions, and so graciously allowed me to do research on site; Forrest Galey, archivist at the Mississippi Department of Archives and History, who meticulously discussed photographs in the Welty Collection with me and directed me as to whom or where I needed to go to obtain the correct permissions; editor/author Patti Carr Black, who shared her personal photographs and whose book *Early Escapades*, about Eudora's youthful writings and illustrations, and the collection she edited for the Mississippi Department of Archives and History, *Eudora*, a wonderful scrapbook of photographs of Eudora's young life—her family, friends, and most importantly, herself—were invaluable sources in the writing of this biography; Dr. Pearl McHaney, who assisted me in putting together the most complete list of Eudora's honors and awards, and worked with me on the list of major adaptations of her works; and Dr. Bridget Pieschel, who so generously shared the presentation she gave at the February 2009 Natchez Literary and Cinema Festival.

In addition, I would like to thank the following agencies and institutions for permission to quote or use materials in their possession: Russell and Volkening Literary Agency, Mississippi Department of

Archives and History, Harvard University Press, Houghton Mifflin Harcourt, and University Press of Mississippi.

I also want to thank my two writing partners, Sarah Campbell and Julie Nolte Owen, who read several versions of the manuscript, and whose comments and insights were extremely valuable; the Welty House staff, who were most gracious in allowing me to work on the premises and helped me in any way they could; and the University Press of Mississippi staff—the director and my editor, Leila Salisbury, assistant director/art director John Langston, and editorial associate Valerie Jones. And thanks to the McRae Foundation for their financial support.

Finally, I am most grateful to my husband, Lus, and my two sons, Will and Sam, who have been patient and understanding while "Mom" has been working. You inspire me every day.

Appendix 1
Eudora Welty's Artwork

As a young girl and into her twenties and thirties, Eudora liked to illustrate. She submitted pictures to her high school yearbook and college humor magazine and annual, as well as *St. Nicholas* magazine and the Memphis *Commercial Appeal*. She also liked to doodle for fun, and even included artwork in letters to her friends. Eudora's excellence in photography is an established fact; however, what is not as well known about her is that she was a very good painter. After her death, the family and staff of the Eudora

A watercolor of Eudora's friend Helen Lotterhos.

Welty House made an amazing discovery: a workman found a large painting by Eudora in the basement of her home. The lively and colorful painting depicts the Mississippi State Fair that comes to Jackson every October. It has been restored and now hangs in the Eudora Welty House Education and Visitors Center. The other examples of her artwork can be be viewed upon request at the Mississippi Department of Archives and History in Jackson.

A scene from Eudora's painting of the Mississippi State Fair.

Eudora included this watercolor angel in a Christmas letter to her agent, Diarmuid Russell, December 1940.

Appendix 2
Chronology of Eudora Welty's Life

1909	On April 13 Eudora Alice Welty born to Christian and Chestina Welty.
1912	Brother Edward born.
1915	Brother Walter born.
1925	Moves into the house at 1119 Pinehurst Place; graduates from Jackson High School.
1925–27	Attends Mississippi State College for Women, Columbus, Mississippi.
1927–29	Attends and graduates from the University of Wisconsin, Madison, Wisconsin.
1930–31	Attends Columbia University School of Business, New York, New York.
1931	Christian Welty dies.
1931–33	Eudora works at WJDX radio station, Jackson, Mississippi.
1936	First photography exhibit at Lugene Opticians, Inc., New York City; "Death of a Traveling Salesman" and "Magic" published in *Manuscript* magazine; works for the Works Progress Administration.
1937–39	Ten stories published in three different magazines: *Southern Review*, *Prairie Schooner*, and *River*.
1940	Eudora hires Diarmuid Russell as agent; he serves as her agent until his death in 1973.
1941	Eudora's first collection of stories, *A Curtain of Green*, is published.

1942	Eudora receives Guggenheim Fellowship but because of World War II stays in Jackson.
1949	Eudora receives second Guggenheim Fellowship and this time uses it to travel to Europe.
1952	Eudora elected to the National Institute of Arts and Letters.
1959	Eudora's brother Walter dies.
1966	In January Eudora's mother, Chestina, and brother, Edward, die, just four days apart.
1972	*The Optimist's Daughter* is published in its revised and expanded form; Eudora receives the Gold Medal for Fiction from the National Institute of Arts and Letters and is elected to the American Academy.
1973	Eudora receives the Pulitzer Prize.
1980	Eudora receives the Presidential Medal of Freedom.
1981	Eudora receives the National Medal of Literature.
1984	*One Writer's Beginnings* is published.
1986	Eudora receives National Medal of the Arts.
1996	Eudora receives the French Legion of Honor.
1998	The Library of America publishes two volumes of Eudora's works, including fiction and nonfiction. "Welty was the first living author to be published in this series, joining greats such as Twain, Irving, Melville and Faulkner."
2001	On July 23 Eudora dies, age ninety-two.

Appendix 3
Books by Eudora Welty

Posthumous Publications

Members of the cast of *The Ponder Heart* at New Stage Theatre in Jackson, 2009.

Appendix 4
Major Adaptations
of Eudora Welty's Works

1952   *Eudora Welty Reading Selections from A Curtain of Green*, Caedmon Records, TS 1010

1955   "The Key," *Jane Wyman Presents The Fireside Theatre* (TV series)

1956   *The Ponder Heart*, Broadway adaptation by Jerome Chodorov and Joseph Fields

1976   *The Robber Bridegroom*, Broadway adaptation by Alfred Uhry

1984   *One Writer's Beginnings: Eudora Welty in Her Own Voice*, set of three CDs, Harvard University Press

1987   *The Wide Net*, directed by Anthony Herrera (TV movie)

1989   *The Hitch-Hikers*, directed by Alan Bergmann (film)

1989   *Eudora Welty: One Writer's Beginnings*, directed by Patchy Wheatley and produced by Patchy Wheatley for the BBC, *The American Experience* (TV series documentary)

1994   *A Worn Path*, directed by Bruce Schwartz (film)

1996   *The Key*, directed by Francis James (film)

1998   *Why I Live at the P.O.*, directed by Jodie Markell (film)

2001   *The Ponder Heart*, directed by Martha Coolidge, *Masterpiece Theatre* (TV movie)

2008   *The Shoe Bird*, choral and orchestral adaptation by Samuel Jones

2008   *The Frost Whistle: An Adaptation of "The Whistle,"* directed by Catherine Owens (film)

2009   *A Visit of Charity*, directed by Tom Ptasinski (film)

2010   *The Purple Hat*, directed by Gregory Doucette (film)

Appendix 5
List of Honorary Degrees and Major Awards

HONORARY DEGREES

1954	Doctor of Letters, University of Wisconsin–Madison
1955	Doctor in Letters, Western College for Women, Ohio
1956	Doctor in Letters, Smith College, Massachusetts
1969	Doctor of Humane Letters, Millsaps College, Mississippi
1971	Doctor of Literature, Denison University, Ohio
1971	Doctor of Letters, The University of the South, Tennessee
1971	Doctor in Letters, Meridian University, California
1972	Doctor of Letters, Washington and Lee University, Virginia
1973	Queens University, North Carolina
1975	Doctor of Letters, Tulane University, Louisiana
1975	Doctor of Humane Letters, Southern Methodist University, Texas
1975	Doctor of Letters, Yale University, Connecticut
1975	Doctor of Literature, Mount Holyoke College, Massachusetts
1976	Doctor of Letters, The University of North Carolina at Chapel Hill
1977	Doctor of Letters, Washington University, Missouri
1977	Doctor of Literature, Harvard University, Massachusetts
1978	Doctor of Letters, Rutgers University, New Jersey
1979	Doctor of Letters, University of Illinois at Urbana-Champaign
1979	Doctor of Humane Letters, Brandeis University, Massachusetts
1980	Doctor of Humanities, Drew University, New Jersey
1980	Doctor of Letters, Belhaven College, Mississippi

1980	Doctor of Letters, Kenyon College, Ohio
1980	Doctor of Humane Letters, Southwestern College at Memphis (Rhodes College)
1980	Doctor of Humanities, Brigham Young University, Utah
1981	Doctor of Humane Letters, Randolph-Macon College, Virginia
1981	Doctor of Literature, William Carey College, Mississippi
1981	Doctor of Literature, University of West Florida, Florida
1982	Doctor of Humane Letters, Columbia University, New York
1982	Doctor of Humane Letters, Emory University, Georgia
1984	Doctor of Letters, Wake Forest University, North Carolina
1985	Doctor of Humane Letters, The College of William and Mary, Virginia
1986	Doctor of Humane Letters, Queens College, New York
1987	Doctor of Letters, University of Charleston, West Virginia
1988	Doctor of Literature, Princeton University, New Jersey
1989	Doctor of Humane Letters, Chestnut Hill College, Pennsylvania
1991	Doctor of Humane Letters, Centenary College, Louisiana
1993	Honorary Doctorate, University of Burgundy, France
1998	Doctor of Humane Letters, Mississippi University for Women

MAJOR AWARDS

1920	Silver Badge, *St. Nicholas* magazine, for the drawing *A Heading for August*
1925	Silver Badge, *St. Nicholas* magazine, for the poem "In the Twilight"
1938	"Lily Daw and the Three Ladies" in *The Best American Short Stories 1938*
1939	"A Curtain of Green" in *The Best American Short Stories 1939*
1939	"Petrified Man" in *Prize Stories 1939: The O. Henry Awards*
1940	"The Hitch-Hikers" in *The Best American Short Stories 1940*
1941	"A Worn Path" in *Prize Stories 1941: The O. Henry Awards*, second place
1942	Guggenheim Fellowship
1942	"The Wide Net" in *Prize Stories 1942: The O. Henry Awards*, first place

1943   "Asphodel" in *The Best American Short Stories 1943*

1943   "Livvie Is Back" in *Prize Stories 1943: The O. Henry Awards*, first place

1944   American Academy of Arts and Letters, $1000 prize

1946   "A Sketching Trip" in *Prize Stories 1946: The O. Henry Awards*

1947   "The Whole World Knows" in *Prize Stories 1947: The O. Henry Awards*

1949   Guggenheim Fellowship renewal

1951   "The Burning" in *Prize Stories 1951: The O. Henry Awards*, second place

1952   Election to the National Institute of Arts and Letters

1955   Howells Medal for Fiction from the American Academy of Arts and Letters for *The Ponder Heart*

1957   "A Flock of Guinea Hens Seen from a Car" in *Best Poems of 1957*

1968   "The Demonstrators" in *Prize Stories 1968: The O. Henry Awards*, first place

1972   Election to the American Academy of Arts and Letters

1972   Gold Medal for Fiction from the National Institute of Arts and Letters

1973   Pulitzer Prize for Fiction for *The Optimist's Daughter*

1980   National Medal for Literature

1980   Presidential Medal of Freedom given by President Jimmy Carter

1984   Commonwealth Award from the Modern Language Association

1984   Elmer Holmes Bobst Award for Fiction for lifetime achievement in arts and letters

1986   National Medal of the Arts for contributions to the nation's culture from the National Endowment for the Arts, given by President Ronald Reagan

1987   French Chevalier de l'Ordre des Arts et Lettres medal

1988   Mississippi Institute of Arts and Letters Lifetime Achievement Award

1989   Selected to have portrait hung in the National Portrait Gallery of the Smithsonian Institution by the National Portrait Gallery Commission

1991   Cleanth Brooks Medal for Distinguished Achievement in Southern Letters from the Fellowship of Southern Writers

1991	National Book Foundation Medal for Distinguished Contribution to American Letters
1991	PEN/Malamud Award for Excellence in the Short Story
1992	Charles Frankel Humanities Prize from the National Endowment for the Humanities
1992	Rea Award for the Short Story
1996	French Legion d'Honneur
1999	Distinguished Achievement Award from the Southern Book Critics Circle

Abbreviations Used in the Notes

CEW	*Conversations with Eudora Welty*
CS	*The Collected Stories of Eudora Welty*
E	*Eudora*
EE	*Early Escapades*
EOS	*The Eye of the Story: Selected Essays and Reviews*
EW	*Eudora Welty: A Biography*
EWCB	"Eudora Welty Centennial Brochure"
EWF	Eudora Welty Foundation website
EWP	*Eudora Welty Photographs*
MCEW	*More Conversations with Eudora Welty*
NBF	*The Norton Book of Friendship*
NYT	*New York Times*
O	*Occasions: Selected Writings*
OWB	*One Writer's Beginnings*
OWI	*One Writer's Imagination*
SSEW	*Selected Stories of Eudora Welty*
WHT	Eudora Welty House Tour
WGT	Eudora Welty House Garden Tour
WTS	*What There Is to Say We Have Said: The Correspondence of Eudora Welty and William Maxwell*

Source Notes

Full citations for the sources can be found in the bibliography.

Chapter One
Life in Jackson: Eudora's Early Years

Page

3   "Learning stamps you": "Listening," OWB, p. 9.

3   "[Miss Johnson] was from": "Listening," OWB, p. 26.

4   "provided its own good": "The Flavor of Jackson," EOS, p. 323.

4   "Two blocks away": "The Little Store," EOS, p. 326.

5   "it was still": "The Little Store," EOS, p. 326.

5   "the old familiars" and "Many Jackson familiars": "Jackson: A Neighborhood," O, p. 146.

5   "I knew even the": "The Little Store," EOS, p. 327.

5   "I'd skipped my": "The Little Store," EOS, p. 327.

7   "Down at a child's eye": "The Little Store," EOS, pp. 330–331.

7   "The happiness of": "The Little Store," EOS, p. 332.

7   "the boys" and "their long-necked banjos": "Learning to See," OWB, p. 52.

8   "Why, Papa gave me that": "Learning to See," OWB, p. 47.

8   "One measure of my love": "Listening," OWB, pp. 8–9.

8   "the mountain roads" and "frozen winter night": "Learning to See," OWB, p. 51.

9   "'Little girl,' he'd said": "Learning to See," OWB, p. 51.

9   "[She] drew me": "Listening," OWB, p. 17.

10   "any room in our": "Listening," OWB, p. 5.

10   "I must have given": "Listening," OWB, p. 5.

10   "I don't remember": "Listening," OWB, p. 21.

11   "spent her life": "Listening," OWB, p. 14.

11   "this was a day": "Listening," OWB, p. 14.

11   "My mother cut": "Listening," OWB, p. 14.

11   "Fannie, I'd rather": "Listening," OWB, p. 14.

11   "didn't bother about": "Listening," OWB, p. 14.

13   "all instruments that": "Listening," OWB, p. 3.

13   "to find the": "Listening," OWB, p. 3.

13   "folding Kodak": "Listening," OWB, p. 3.

13   "inscribed on the": "Finding a Voice," OWB, p. 81.

14   "little red Royal": "Finding a Voice," OWB, p. 81.

Chapter Two

Eudora's Education

15   "The pleasures of": "A Sweet Devouring," EOS, p. 281.

15   "knowledge of the": "Listening," OWB, p. 9.

15   "They taught it": "Listening," OWB, p. 9.

15   "I fell in love": "Listening," OWB, p. 9.

16   "Indeed, my parents": "Listening," OWB, p. 8.

16   "There were many": "A Sweet Devouring," EOS, p. 280.

16   "[s]he called me": "A Sweet Devouring," EOS, p. 281.

17   "I coasted": "A Sweet Devouring," EOS, p. 281.

17   "My mother" and "Oh, all right": "Listening," OWB, p. 22.

17   "a lifelong": "Listening," OWB, p. 22.

17   "Her standards": "Listening," OWB, 23.

18   "I offered up": "Listening," OWB, pp. 25–26.

18   "improve in poetry" J.H. W_____, Mackie Pine Oil Specialty
      Co., 29 August 1921, Welty Collection.

19   "Once Upon a Time": *St. Nicholas* magazine, p. 108.

19   "In the Twilight": *St. Nicholas* magazine, p. 328.

20   "It was Jackson High": EE, p. 12.

20   "over twenty pen-": EE, p. 18.

20   "at least five": EE, p. 13.

20   "Dearest": EE, p. 17.

20   "author": EE, p. 18.

22 "Chessie and Chris": EW, p. 15.

23 "Within five months": EE, p. 22.

23 "Egged on by": EE, pp. 23–24.

24 "life in a crowd" and "We'd fight": "Finding a Voice," OWB, p. 77.

25 "I walked into": "Finding a Voice," OWB, p. 80.

25 "brilliant" and "an usually": Ricardo Quintana, 3 September 1929, Welty Collection.

25 "I read 'Sailing'": "Finding a Voice," OWB, p. 81.

27 "It was the": Eudora Welty to Diarmuid Russell, 30 September 1941, Welty Collection.

27 "Despite her": EW, p. 22.

Chapter Three
The 1930s: Finding Her Eye and Her Voice

28 "Writing 'Death of'": "Finding a Voice," OWB, p. 87.

29 "was enchanted" and "I was the": EE, p. 32.

29 "When my father": "Finding a Voice," OWB, pp. 92–93.

30 "Eudora would be": EW, p. 36.

30 "She was the": EE, p. 36.

31 "How I would": Eudora Welty to *New Yorker*, 15 March 1933, *New Yorker* Archive.

32 "My brother Edward": Introduction, EWP, p. xiii.

32 "photographed everything": Eudora Welty to Berenice Abbott, 9 August 1934, collection of Suzanne Marrs.

33 "Without any hesitation": John Rood to Eudora Welty, 19 March 1936, Welty Collection.

33 "That was a": Interview with Jane Reid Petty, CEW, p. 208.

34 "junior publicity": Introduction, EWP, p. xxv.

34 "I was sent": "One Time, One Place," EOS, p. 349.

34 "I was so": Interview with Bill Ferris, CEW, p. 155.

35 "I simply": "One Time, One Place," EOS, p. 351.

36 "How did" and "I didn't": Introduction, EWP, p. xxvi.

36 "the whole of," "he showed me," and "he'd never got": Introduction, EWP, p. xxvii.

36   "a perfect" and "The good": Introduction, EWP, p. xxv.

36   "about a little": EW, p. 53.

Chapter Four
Before the War: Friends, Fellowship, and Early Success

37   "I haven't a literary": Introduction, SSEW, p. xiii.

37   "I had sent it": Interview with Tom Royals and John Little, CEW, p. 257.

38   "What Eudora the": EW, pp. 53–54.

38   "The next morning" and "a new insight": EW, p. 58.

38   "Death of a"": O, p. 300.

38   "A neighbor of": "Looking Back at the First Story," O, p. 300.

39   "Creating a garden": "The Perfect Garden," collection of Suzanne Marrs.

41   "Don't take it": OWI, p. 9.

41   "In a little": Introduction, EWP, p. xxiii.

43   "Even when we": Introduction, EWP, p. xxi.

43   "played a variety": EE, p. 39 and EW, p. 47.

43   "the only white": EW, p. 47.

43   "transformed her": EW, p. 66.

44   "Lilies that fester": Sonnet 94, William Shakespeare.

44   "We did it": "That Bright Face Is Laughing, for Robert W. Daniel, 1983," O, p. 207.

44   "Yes, Be my": Eudora Welty to Diarmuid Russell, 31 May 1940, Welty Collection.

44   "Such promptness": Diarmuid Russell to Eudora Welty, 3 June 1940, Welty Collection.

45   "It was just": Eudora Welty to Diarmuid Russell, 30 September 1941, Welty Collection.

45   "If you keep": Eudora Welty to Diarmuid Russell, 5 November 1940, Welty Collection.

47   "very fine work": Katherine Anne Porter to Eudora Welty, 25 October 1938, Welty Collection.

47 "She gets her right": Introduction, SSEW, p. xiii.

48 "Normal social life": Introduction, SSEW, pp. xii–xiii.

Chapter Five
World War II: A Promising Career Interrupted

49 "Do you think this at": Eudora Welty to John Robinson, 13 July 1944, Welty Collection.

49 "Are big bombers": Eudora Welty to Diarmuid Russell, 20 September 1941, Welty Collection.

50 "a mark" and "of their growing": EW, p. 80.

50 "which had brought": EW, p. 85.

50 "Eudora would write": EW, p. 90.

51 "treat[ing] these men": EW, p. 98.

52 "dramatic irony" and "She and her": EW, p. 129.

52 "I hope this": Eudora Welty to Diarmuid Russell, 13 August 1945, Welty Collection.

52 "Dear Sir:": "Voice of the People, Letter against Gerald L. K. Smith," Letter to the Editor, *Clarion-Ledger*, Jackson, Mississippi, December 20, 1945, O, pp. 223–224.

53 "got some phone calls": Eudora Welty to Diarmuid Russell, n.d. (late December 1945), Welty Collection.

53 "out for your blood": Diarmuid Russell to Eudora Welty, 2 January 1946, Welty Collection.

54 "After the Meudon party": Eudora Welty to Frank Lyell, 16 January 1950, Welty Collection.

57 "It really is": Eudora Welty to Diarmuid Russell, 20 July 1953, Welty Collection.

58 "All I can really": Eudora Welty to Frank Lyell, 3 November 1952, Welty Collection.

58 "What Stevenson Started," from the January 5, 1953, issue of the *New Republic*, appears in full in O, pp. 229–231.

Chaper Six
The 1960s: Personal and Political Unrest

59   "What I do in": Preface to CS, p. xi.

61   "It's still incredible": Eudora Welty to Frank Lyell, n.d. (January 1959), Welty Collection.

61   "Heavens, Elizabeth": ibid.

61   "[D]angerously inadequate": EW, p. 279.

62   "Such awful things": Eudora Welty to Diarmuid Russell, 25 September 1957, Welty Collection.

63   "such hostility": EW, p. 304.

63   "I can't even": Eudora Welty to Frank Lyell, 10 December 1963, Welty Collection.

64   "Mother is in": Eudora Welty to Mary Lou Aswell, 25 March 1964, Welty Collection.

64   "My class at": Eudora Welty to Bill Smith, n.d., collection of Suzanne Marrs.

65   "What matters": "Must the Novelist Crusade?," EOS, pp. 152–153.

65   "It deals with" and "Mr. Forster,": "Must the Novelist Crusade?," EOS, p. 154.

66   "Eudora called attention": EW, p. 314.

66   "[T]hank you": WTS, p. 186.

Chapter Seven
Grief and Recovery: *The Optimist's Daughter* and
One Writer's Beginnings

67   "Of course the": "Finding a Voice," OWB, p. 104.

68   "may be grim": Eudora Welty to Frank Lyell, 18 February 1967, Welty Collection.

68   "such memories": EW, p. 332.

69   "Such a wonderful": Eudora Welty to Ken Millar, 30 March 1973, Welty Collection.

70   "repeatedly stress her": EW, p. 403.

70   "Writing was not": EW, p. 403.

71   "A writer's autobiography": EW, pp. 446–447.

71   "The audience was": Bill Maxwell, "The Charged Imagination," 20 February 1984, *New Yorker* Archive.

72   "Eudora's wry wit": EW, pp. 481–482.

72   "There was dialogue": "Listening," OWB, p. 13.

72   "Long before I": "Listening," OWB, p. 14.

73   "The trips were": "Learning to See," OWB, p. 68.

73   "The events in": "Learning to See," OWB, pp. 68–69.

74   "In the midst": EW, pp. 485–486.

74   "[S]elf-portraits and portraits": EW, p. 486.

Chapter Eight
The Importance of Friendship: Eudora's Final Days

75   "Lately in my": Introduction, NBF, 40.

77   "Perhaps she lacked": EW, p. 488.

77   "[F]riendships were at": EW, p. 527.

77   "I'm stage-struck" and "I'm absolutely": "A Male Bastion Bows, in Gracious Greeting," NYT, p. 2.

78   "From five feet": EW, pp. 545–546.

79   "The reading and": EW, p. 549.

80   "I think what": Interview with Joseph Dumas, MCEW, pp. 282–285.

80   "felt that a production": EW, p. 553.

80   "Is Phoenix Jackson's": "Is Phoenix Jackson's Grandson Really Dead?," EOS, p. 159.

80   "No": EW, p. 553.

80   "Eudora was more": EW, p. 557.

81   "[she] now faced": EW, p. 559.

81   "During these last": EW, p. 559.

82   "for the purpose": WHT, p. 3.

82   "The speakers and": EW, p. 568.

82   "she knew me,": EW, pp. 569–570.

84   "Burial took place": EW, pp. 570–571.

Afterword
Eudora Welty's House

85   "in giving it": EWF, p. 1.
85   "in preserving": EWCB.
85   "it is one of": EWF, p. 1.
87   "they would have to": WHT, p. 3.
88   "She did not": WHT, p. 7.
88   "the original cut": WHT, p. 3.
88   "show garden": WGT, p. 2.
88   "she viewed the": WGT, p. 2.

Photo Captions

2   "the first": E, p. 39.
13   "Edward and I": E, p. 35.
46   "[T]hat summer": E, p. 61.

Appendix 2
Chronology of Eudora Welty's Life

96   "Welty was the": WHT, 3.

Bibliography

WORKS BY EUDORA WELTY

The Collected Stories of Eudora Welty. New York: Harcourt, 1980.

Early Escapades. Ed. Patti Carr Black. Jackson: University Press of Mississippi, 2005.

Eudora. Ed. Patti Carr Black. Jackson: Mississippi Department of Archives and History, 1984.

"The Flavor of Jackson." Originally published as the "Introduction" to *The Jackson Cookbook*, 1971. Reprinted in *The Eye of the Story.* New York: Vintage, 1990. 321–325.

"In the Twilight." *St. Nicholas* magazine, January 1925. 328.

"Introduction." *The Norton Book of Friendship.* Ed. Eudora Welty and Ronald Sharp. New York: Norton, 1991.

"Is Phoenix Jackson's Grandson Really Dead?" Originally published in *Critical Inquiry*, University of Chicago Press, No. 1, September 1974. Reprinted in *The Eye of the Story.* New York: Vintage, 1990. 159–162.

"Jackson: A Neighborhood." Originally published in *Jackson Landmarks*, ed. Linda Thompson Greaves et al., Jackson: The Junior League of Jackson, 1982. Reprinted in *Occasions: Selected Writings*, ed. Pearl A. McHaney. Jackson: University Press of Mississippi, 2009. 145–150.

"The Little Store." Originally published as "The Corner Store," *Esquire*, December 1975. Reprinted in *The Eye of the Story.* New York: Vintage, 1990. 326–335.

"Looking Back at the First Story." Originally published in the *Georgia Review*, winter 1979. Reprinted in *Occasions: Selected Writings*, ed. Pearl A. McHaney. Jackson: University Press of Mississippi, 2009. 299–305.

"Must the Novelist Crusade?" Originally published in the *Atlantic*, October 1965. Reprinted in *The Eye of the Story.* New York: Vintage, 1990. 146–158.

"Once Upon a Time." *St. Nicholas* magazine, November 1923, 108.

"One Time, One Place." Originally published by Random House, 1970. Excerpts reprinted in *The Eye of the Story*. New York: Vintage, 1990. 349–355.

One Writer's Beginnings. Cambridge: Harvard University Press, 2003.

The Optimist's Daughter. New York: Vintage, 1990.

Photographs. Jackson: University Press of Mississippi, 1989.

Selected Stories of Eudora Welty. New York: Modern Library, 1971.

"Shadows." *Wisconsin Literary Magazine*, April 1928, 34. Reprinted with permission of EW, LLC.

"A Sweet Devouring." Originally published in *Mademoiselle*, 1957. Reprinted in *The Eye of the Story*. New York: Vintage, 1990. 279–285.

"That Bright Face Is Laughing." Originally published in the *Kenyon Review*, 5 new series, spring 1983. Reprinted in *Occasions: Selected Writings*, ed. Pearl A. McHaney. Jackson: University Press of Mississippi, 2009. 206–207.

"Voice of the People, Letter against Gerald L. K. Smith." Originally published in the Jackson *Clarion-Ledger*, 23 December 1945. Reprinted in *Occasions: Selected Writings*, ed. Pearl A. McHaney. Jackson: University Press of Mississippi, 2009. 223–224.

"What Stevenson Started." Originally published in the *New Republic*, 5 January 1953. Reprinted in *Occasions: Selected Writings*, ed. Pearl A. McHaney. Jackson: University Press of Mississippi, 2009. 229–231.

LETTERS FROM EUDORA WELTY TO:

Abbott, Berenice. Photocopy. Private collection of Suzanne Marrs.

Aswell, Mary Lou. Welty (Eudora Alice) Collection. Mississippi Department of Archives and History, Jackson, Mississippi.

Lyell, Frank. Welty (Eudora Alice) Collection. Mississippi Department of Archives and History, Jackson, Mississippi.

Millar, Kenneth and Margaret. Welty (Eudora Alice) Collection. Mississippi Department of Archives and History, Jackson, Mississippi.

Robinson, John F. Private collection of Michael Robinson. Welty (Eudora Alice) Collection. Mississippi Department of Archives and History, Jackson, Mississippi.

Russell, Diarmuid. Welty (Eudora Alice) Collection. Mississippi Department of Archives and History, Jackson, Mississippi.

Smith, Bill. Photocopy. Private collection of Suzanne Marrs.

Letters to Eudora Welty Held by the Mississippi Department
of Archives and History, Welty (Eudora Alice) Collection:

Porter, Katherine Anne
Quintana, Ricardo
Rood, John
Russell, Diarmuid
W———., J. H., Mackie Pine Oil Specialty Co.

OTHER ARCHIVAL MATERIAL

Welty, Chestina. "The Perfect Garden." Photocopy. Personal collection of Suzanne Marrs.

Welty Family Photographs. Welty Family Photo Album. Welty (Eudora Alice) Collection. Mississippi Department of Archives and History, Jackson, Mississippi.

Welty Family Photographs. Personal collection of Mary Alice Welty White and Elizabeth Welty Thompson.

OTHER SOURCES

Burger, Nash K., with Pearl A. McHaney. *The Road to West 43rd Street.* Jackson: University Press of Mississippi, 1995.

Collins, Glenn. "A Male Bastion Bows, in Gracious Greeting." *New York Times*, 22 April 1989. http://www.nytimes.com/1989/04/22/arts/a-male-bastion-bows-in-gracious-greeting.html.

Eudora Welty Foundation. http://www.eudorawelty.org/foundation.html.

Eudora Welty House. http://www.eudorawelty.org./house.html.

Marrs, Suzanne. *Eudora Welty: A Biography.* New York: Harcourt, 2005.

———. "Eudora Welty 1909–2001: Celebrating the Centennial of Miss Welty's Birth." Jackson, MS: Millsaps College, 2009.

————. *One Writer's Imagination: The Fiction of Eudora Welty.* Baton Rouge: Louisiana State University Press, 2002.

————, ed. *What There Is to Say We Have Said: The Correspondence of Eudora Welty and William Maxwell.* Boston: Houghton Mifflin Harcourt, 2011.

Maxwell, William. "The Charged Imagination." *New Yorker,* 20 February 1984, 133–135. http://archives.newyorker.com.

Pieschel, Bridget. "Voices from 'A World to Itself,' Eudora Welty's Mississippi Women's Microcosm." Presented at the Natchez Literary and Cinema Festival, February 2009.

Prenshaw, Peggy, ed. *Conversations with Eudora Welty.* Jackson: University Press of Mississippi, 1984.

————, ed. *More Conversations with Eudora Welty.* Jackson: University Press of Mississippi, 1996.

Credits

TEXT CREDITS

Excerpts from the following letters are reprinted by permission of the Eudora Welty Collection–Mississippi Department of Archives and History and of Russell and Volkening, Inc., as agents for Eudora Welty, LLC, copyright © Eudora Welty, LLC, 1921, 1929, 1936, 1938, 1940, 1941, 1944, 1945, 1946, 1950, 1952, 1953, 1957, 1959, 1963, 1964, 1967, 1973.

FROM EUDORA WELTY:

To Mary Lou Aswell: 25 March 1964
To Frank Lyell: 16 January 1950; 3 November 1952; n.d. (January) 1959; 10 December 1963; 18 February 1967
To Ken Millar: 30 March 1973
To John Robinson: 13 July 1944
To Diarmuid Russell: 31 May 1940; 5 November 1940; 20 September 1941; 30 September 1941; 13 August 1945; n.d. (late December) 1945; 2 January 1946; 20 July 1953; 25 September 1957

TO EUDORA WELTY:

From Katherine Anne Porter: 25 October 1938
From John Rood: 19 March 1936
From Diarmuid Russell: 3 June 1940; 2 January 1946
From J. H. W_____, Mackie Pine Oil Specialty Co., 29 August 1921

OTHER:

Ricardo Quintana, 3 September 1929

Excerpts reprinted by permission of the publisher from *One Writer's Beginnings* by Eudora Welty, pp. 3, 5, 8–9, 13, 14, 17, 21, 22, 23, 25–26, 47, 51, 52, 68–69, 77, 80, 81, 87, 92–93, 104, Cambridge, Mass.: Harvard University Press, Copyright © 1983, 1984 by Eudora Welty.

Excerpts from *Eudora Welty: A Biography* copyright © 2005 by Suzanne Marrs, reprinted by permission of Houghton Mifflin Harcourt Publishing Company.

Excerpts from *Eudora Welty: Photographs* are reprinted by permission of University Press of Mississippi.

Excerpts from the introduction to *Early Escapades* by Eudora Welty are reprinted by permission of the editor, Patti Carr Black.

Excerpts from letters and papers in the private collection of Suzanne Marrs are reprinted courtesy of the owner: Eudora Welty to Berenice Abbott, 9 August 1934; "The Perfect Garden," Chestina Welty; Eudora Welty to Bill Smith, n.d.

ILLUSTRATION CREDITS

Illustrations on the following pages are reprinted by the permission of the Eudora Welty Collection–Mississippi Department of Archives and History and of Russell and Volkening, Inc., as agents for Eudora Welty, LLC, copyright © Eudora Welty, LLC: 2, 4, 6, 10, 11, 12, 13, 14, 16, 17, 21, 22, 29, 30, 33, 34, 35, 36, 39, 40, 41, 42 (bottom right), 44, 46, 60 (top left), 88, 94

Illustrations on the following pages are reprinted by the permission of Russell and Volkening, Inc., as agents for Eudora Welty, LLC, copyright © Eudora Welty, LLC: 18, 21, 22, 24, 26, 29, 31, 41, 42 (middle and left bottom),

43, 51, 54, 55, 56, 57, 58, 60 (top and bottom right), 61, 68, 69, 74, 76, 78, 81, 87, 92, 93

The photograph of Eudora Welty in the *Meh Lady* yearbook is reprinted courtesy of Mississippi State College for Women and Eudora Welty, LLC.

The photograph of Eudora Welty on the campus of Mississippi State College for Women was taken by Norma Cox.

The photograph of Eudora Welty from the Badger Yearbook is reprinted courtesy of the UW Madison Archives and Eudora Welty, LLC.

The photograph of the night-blooming cereus is reprinted courtesy of Mary Alice Welty White.

The photograph of Eudora Welty in Italy was taken by Barbara Howes and is reprinted courtesy of Gregory Smith and Eudora Welty, LLC.

The photograph of Chestina Welty in the 1950s was taken by Rollie McKenna.

The photograph of Medgar Evers is reprinted courtesy of University Press of Mississippi.

The photograph of Eudora Welty working with a student at Millsaps College is reprinted courtesy of Millsaps College Archives.

The photograph of Eudora Welty's copy of E. M. Forster's *A Passage to India* and the photograph of Eudora Welty's painting of the Mississippi State Fair are reprinted by permission of the Collection of the Museum Division, Mississippi Department of Archives and History.

The photographs of Eudora Welty on her way to Europe, in Paris, and at her eightieth birthday party are reprinted courtesy of Patti Carr Black.

The photograph of Eudora Welty and Jim Lehrer was taken by Chuck Allen and is reprinted courtesy of New Stage Theatre and Eudora Welty, LLC.

The photographs of the crowd paying their respects to the Welty family at the Old Capitol Museum in Jackson (photographer Suzi Altman) and of Eudora Welty's living room (photographer Gretchen Hain) are reprinted by permission of the Collection of the Office of Public Information, Mississippi Department of Archives and History.

The photographs of the Eudora Welty House today (photographer Karen Redhead), the living room bookcase, the display cases inside the Eudora Welty House Education and Visitors Center, and the cast of New Stage Theater in Jackson are reprinted courtesy of the Mississippi Department of Archives and History.

The photograph of Eudora Welty and Suzanne Marrs was taken by Nancy Ellis and is reprinted courtesy of Suzanne Marrs.

The photographs of the Library of America volumes and of Eudora's gravestone were taken by Richard Campbell.

Index